*Reflections
of a
Miracle*

Copyright © 2007 Anthony Mucciacciaro
All Rights Reserved

ISBN-10:   1-934478-05-9
ISBN-13:   978-1-934478-05-9

Content of this book are the exclusive property of the author. No part of this book may be used or reproduced in any manner whatsoever without written permission except in the case of brief quotations embodied in critical articles or book reviews.

The author may be contacted at:

        reflectionsofamiracle@hotmail.com

Printed in the United States of America by
Sunray Publishing Solutions, St. Cloud, Minnesota

Dedicated to:

the addicts who are still suffering

Anthony Mucciaccaro

CHAPTER ONE

My name is Antonio and this is my reflections of a miracle.

I was born in Memorial Hospital in San Jose, California on February 17, 1963. I am one of eleven children of my father. I am one of five of my mother. Let me explain. My mother was married before and had a son, then she married my father and had three sons and one daughter. My father was married three times that I am aware of. He was married to a woman in Alaska and had three girls whom I have never met. Next he married my mother and had four children. His third marriage was to a woman who already had a son of her own, and then she and my father had four more sons.

Are there more? I believe there may be, but I'll never really know, unless they all step forward. Who would really want to be associated with a family history such as this? As you can see my childhood was not very stable. I would often wake up at different family members' homes - at an aunt's or uncle's house. Then my parents bought a farm in Clearlake, Wisconsin. My first memory of my dad was when I was four or five years of age. When my dad came home I ran to him to give him a hug as I had seen other kids do on TV. Instead of a hug my dad began to beat me. I started to cry, but no noise came out. He just would not stop. My mom tried to intercede to protect me and my dad started beating her. I ran and hid from him underneath the stair case. I heard him hitting mom, and as she crawled by me, her glasses fell off her face. She crawled about four feet past me as I was hiding underneath the stairwell.

I remember climbing out a few hours later. My mom's blood-stained glasses were still on the floor and as I picked them up the lens popped out. I didn't know what to do, so I went to mom to try to comfort her, but she only moaned. I was very angry and confused. I kept asking God to help me because I didn't know what to do. I was scared, and I didn't know what I had done wrong. It became a daily task to comfort my mom after she had been beaten by my father. Some days only mom was beaten. Other days we all were. It was not long afterwards that my mom disappeared.

After my mom and dad divorced, my dad remarried and a new step-mom moved in. This woman was vicious. She was much like a stop light, and you never knew when the light would switch. One minute she liked us and the next she was laughing as we were beaten by our father. She even encouraged our father to beat us more and actually told him lies so we would get beaten. When my dad beat us, it was never with his hands. It could be a board, a stick, a wire, a shovel, a broom, a hammer, a hose, a door or a chair. When it was over you didn't know how bad it was until you tried to move.

I remember feeling love from my mom, not much but a little bit, and I kept waiting for some love and compassion from my step-mom, but it never came. The best way I can describe this lady is if hell is as bad as they say it is, being there would be a breath of fresh air compared to being with this woman. She gave cruel a whole new meaning. The devil could take lessons from her. The things that woman did are unspeakable, so much so that I can't even write about them. Try to imagine the worst things possible, multiply that by a million and you're not even close. There were unspeakable acts of sexual abuse, torture and flat out monstrous behavior. They say God put everyone on earth for a reason, but I'm positive that the devil himself sent my step-mom and my father first class tickets to come here.

I remember one hot summer day our dog, Bella, cut her foot really bad on a fence. I found my brother sitting in the driveway holding the dog and crying. Seeing us, my father who was cutting hay, stopped the tractor and came over to us. He took a hammer that we used to drive pins out of the tractor hitch, grabbed the dog by its throat and proceeded to strike it in the head several times. Blood was shooting everywhere, even on us. The dog was shaking really hard. Then she stopped. My Dad started walking toward the barn where Bella had delivered five puppies just days before. He told us to drag the dead dog with us to the barn. I was so scared I could barely breathe. I had blood dripping off my face and clothes. Dad walked into the barn where the puppies were. He picked up one puppy at a time and threw it on the floor. He killed all five pups right in front of us. Afterwards he picked up all six dogs and threw them in the pig pen. The next day Bella and her pups were gone.

There were times that I got hurt playing on the farm. I remember one of those times quite clearly. I was climbing on a barbwire fence to get to an apple tree on the other side. As I climbed over the wire, my foot slipped and a piece of the barbwire stuck in my leg and cut it wide open. I was bleeding really bad and there was a hole in my pants. I couldn't tell Dad I was hurt. I knew he would beat me for sure for climbing on the fence. So I went to the outhouse, rolled up some toilet paper like a cigarette, and laid it in the wound on my leg. I then wrapped a lot of toilet paper around my leg and walked home. I had to take a bath that night but couldn't use toilet paper to fix my leg again. I went out later to feed my dog, Lassie. With blood running down my leg, I stopped at the tractor and took a big wad of grease off the tractor and stuck it in my wound to stop the bleeding. Every night for a week I did that and it finally healed. My dad never knew I cut my leg on the barbwire.

Everyday of my life my dad beat me and my brothers. On the days we didn't do anything, and he knew we had done nothing, he beat us anyway just to make sure because he didn't want to miss anything. My dad didn't beat with just his hands. He used anything laying around that was handy. He left welts so big on our legs that we wouldn't even go swimming during swimming class at school. Then the teachers would call and tell my dad we weren't participating, and because we weren't participating my dad would beat us again.

I remember the first day I went to school. My dad took me to kindergarten and I was screaming and crying and didn't want to leave my dad's side. My dad hit me so hard that I blacked out. I don't remember much of what happened. From that moment on I was unable to learn anything in school because every time the sun rose, I knew my dad would get up and that was very scary for me because I didn't know what he was capable of doing next. The little world I lived in it was very scary and hard, and I begged God to get me out. There were times that my younger brother and I tried to end our lives together. We would take cord from the hay baler, tie knots in it and swallow the knots. We would hold the rope as our bodies trashed around and hoped we would never wake up as we passed out.

I remember swallowing glass and tacks in hopes of dying, but that prayer was never answered either. I didn't know what to do, who to tell, or where to go or anything. All I knew was that when I was at school, my dad couldn't hurt me. So I went there and goofed off because I didn't know how to learn. I was too scared of what was going to happen to me.

I took a candy bar one time from someone at school, and my dad found out about it and beat me. After he beat me he went to the store and bought a case of full size candy bars. It was just a little snack candy bar that I had taken, but my dad made me eat every single candy bar from that case even though I began throwing up. He kept making me eat them to teach me a lesson – guess that is what it was called. After that I was so sick but still had to go to school the next day. None of us kids, my two brothers or me, were allowed to go downstairs to go to the bathroom, so most of the time we were upstairs peeing in each other's hands and drinking it because we were afraid of what was going to happen to us if we went downstairs.

We weren't really good at taking care of things like wiping well when we used the toilet. My dad would beat us if we had an accident in our underwear. He found five pairs of underwear with poop on them that I had hidden under my bed. I was hiding them so I wouldn't get beaten. After finding them, he beat all of us. He hit me until I was unconscious. After that beating whenever there were stains in my underwear I would suck the stain out so my step-mom wouldn't find it and tell my dad.

My dad would beat us for almost anything. One time I reached over the table to grab the milk and my dad hit me so hard with a big fork that he left a big gash on my head. When I went to school the next day, they asked me what happened and I told them that I fell down. Once my dad and I were in the barn milking cows. I was holding the milker against a cow when my step mom came in. She stuck her hand down my pants and fondled me. She smiled at my dad like it was a good thing that she was doing. That night my step-mom came into my room and fondled me again. She also made me fondle her. My dad heard me cry out and he got so mad at me that he beat me and beat me and beat me. I just sat there crying and crying. Everyday became scarier and scarier.

One time I had a Zippo lighter in my hand that I had found down stairs. I was opening it and flicking it when I heard someone coming upstairs to my room. I quickly threw the lighter underneath the bed. Unfortunately it caught the room on fire. My dad ran up and down the stairs throwing water on the fire to keep the house from burning down. The fire department came out and we were able to put the fire out. My dad had broken his leg while running up and down the stairs but still managed to beat me. He hit me six times that I remember, but after that I don't remember anything. My dad could hit so hard and so much that most of the time I would scream for the first few seconds, but after that I was just numb or in shock and couldn't feel anything. My brothers and I knew better than to cry out when we were beaten, but sometimes it hurt so bad you tried to make noise but couldn't. The silence of the scream was devastating. The desperation to scream was beyond anything I'd ever felt in my life.

Finally the day came when my dad decided we were too much for him and our step-mom to put up with. So they put us on an airplane to San Jose, California. I was eight years old and had never flown on an airplane before. Ironically enough they put us on an airplane on October 31, 1972. It was Halloween night, the end of our terror or so I thought. When we walked off the plane, a lady walked up to us and said she was our mom. I hadn't seen my mom since I was six years old, so when she said she was my mom that was good enough for me. I went with her. After the last beating my mom got from my dad, he sent her on "vacation" with my oldest half brother to California to visit her family.

While my mom was there my dad served her divorce papers. I never knew any of that until I was reunited with her that Halloween night.

REFLECTIONS OF A MIRACLE

Chapter Two

My mom had married a man named Clarence King, an elderly man and very rich. They had very beautiful things likes leather couches in their house. They called it the "the big house". It was huge. One time we had a nine-teen foot Christmas tree in the living room. It was just wonderful, like a fairy tale.

After a short time, maybe six weeks or so of living in "the big house", mom asked me if we were alright because we always seemed so scared. After hearing about the way our dad had treated us, my step-dad decided that I was so timid that he figured he could move in and molest me and I would never tell. When my step-dad began sexually molesting me, he did it almost every single night for three years. He did things to me that were so vulgar that I can't even mention them. I never want to hear or feel them again.

Once I tied a rope from my brother's foot to mine so he would wake up my brother when he came in to get me. I hoped tying our feet together would keep my step dad in check, but he brought scissors the next time. What I was going through was devastating.

REFLECTIONS OF A MIRACLE

One day after getting my report card with all failing grades, my older brother came up to me and asked what was wrong. Why couldn't I learn? Mom was all upset. So I told my brother that I was being molested, and he took me to the police department. I was taken into a room with eight officers, four uniformed and four plain clothed. When I sat down and told them the story of what had happened and what my step-dad was doing to me, the four uniformed officers just dipped their heads and walked out. The other officers in the room were looking out the window, one was leaning against the wall and one was writing on a piece of paper. He stopped and stared open-mouthed at me. His pencil wasn't moving anymore.

One officer asked if I was hungry and I said yes. He got me a coke and a hamburger. I didn't like coke, but I drank it anyway. Later they took me back to "the big house" to get my things. I was so angry. I now knew all the things my step-dad was doing to me was wrong. I knew my step-dad kept a loaded shot gun in the entry closet. I grabbed that gun and went after him. I got one shot off before the officer stopped me. I missed my step-dad and shot the wall. My step-dad was arrested and charged. I was given up as a ward of the state. I was taken to a place called Capp Memorial Hospital in San Jose, California, for a mental evaluation.

Chapter Three

Capp Memorial Hospital was more of a nightmare than my real dad and my step-dad put together. The beatings, raping, and sodomizing I received from the staff in that place was unbelievable. I had no one to protect me. Every other day I was getting hit with a shot of thorazine or forced to drink something that tasted nasty. I didn't understand it. There were times I didn't eat for days. There were times I was beaten so badly that I couldn't breathe. My urethra was damaged five times. Once I saw a doctor because I was bleeding from my rectum. The doctor asked me what had happened and I told him I didn't know, I woke up and I was like this.

After this, I was put into a padded room, I guess like a quite time room or whatever. Three people held me down, and a woman pulled my pants down and gave me a shot, most likely thorazine. I remember being pushed around and my body being used, things happening to me. I could feel things. I couldn't stay conscious. I think I was out for two days.

REFLECTIONS OF A MIRACLE

When I woke up in my room there was a new guy that had been brought in. He became violent and knocked out a two inch thick plexi-glass window. The staff shut the place down and locked us all in our rooms. While I was in my room a guy came in and picked me up off the bed and threw me on the floor. He picked me up again and again throwing me to the floor until finally he broke three of my fingers. When he realized that, he left me alone.

He went to the next room and beat on that person. Everyone got beaten that day because of the guy who knocked out that window.

I listened to a song all the time called *Wild Fire* by Michael Martin Murphey. I liked to think of it as getting away and getting free, getting somewhere where people wouldn't hurt me. I wondered if a place like that even existed.

One night after having been raped, I sat in the dark and asked God to kill me. I really truly begged Him to take my life. I prayed that the next time they came in and abused me, they would be so mad and go too far and accidentally break my neck and kill me. Obviously those prayers were never answered.

After about two weeks in that place a lady came in and said her name was Liz DeChristdeforo. She was very pretty. I believed her when she said she was going to help me. I had only heard those words twice in my life, once when the police said it and now this lady was saying it. I was desperate to get out of this place so when the lady said she had a ranch she wanted me to go see, I said I would go. She told me the ranch was really nice. There was a river, cabins, ponies, lots of kids, a playground, and I could have a bike there. So I went.

I want you to remember that in the mean time there had been no schooling for me. I know now that I had gone to public school for a short time. I have a few documents to prove that. Years later my wife called to have those records sent to us, but there were no public records of me in school so they sent my little brother's information.

Clearwater Ranch was in Philo, California. What a place! We pulled up and Liz and I got out with my bag and box. Everywhere I looked, I could hear kids laughing and playing. Liz hugged me. It was a warm loving hug. It was nice to feel that. Liz said, "I'll see you later. Be good. I will check on you from time to time. When your Mom gets it together with a home and everything, we will get you back to her." I said, "Okay." It sounded good.

Liz got back in her car and left. I watched her drive up a little hill and then make a right turn at the foot of the mountain. When her tail lights went out of sight, I felt a blow from behind as if I had been hit by a train. My face hit the ground and I was being dragged backwards by my feet. I could feel gravel cutting my face and going into my mouth. I was dragged to a cabin where I was picked up and thrown against a bed. I think I broke four ribs. I couldn't breathe deeply for three weeks after that.

A man told me to unpack my stuff, sit on the bed and don't move. That's exactly what I did. I was so frightened it wasn't even funny. Life was suppose to get better, and that wasn't exactly working out. It looked like it was going to get a whole lot worse for me and it did.

A guy named Drake was running the place and another guy named Collin took care of us. He was such a vicious man it wasn't even funny. About three or four hours after I was dragged to my room, a man walked back in and asked me if I was hungry and I said yes. He said that was too bad and walked back out.

I sat straight up on that bed for three days and nights. I would fall asleep, and when I did a man was there to smack me. Every time I fell asleep, I got hit. I urinated and defecated in my pants for the first five days I was there. They finally let me get up the fifth or sixth day to take a bath. I got to eat a hamburger. It was cold, but I didn't care. I ate it. I was starving.

Three or four weeks into this place, it wasn't getting any better, and I was scared. I didn't really know what to think of life anymore. For the eleven years of my life so far there had been nothing but torture in one form or another. Was this the end of life? Was this how my life was going to be? Is this what God intended for me? All I knew was these people came in to my room and wanted to hurt me. I heard a lot of kids screaming and screaming all night long. All I could think of was when was this going to end, and when were they going to hurt someone really bad?

One day a man came in and told me to take off my clothes and get in the tub. I thought maybe I hadn't cleaned myself good enough. I did what he told me. I was standing there in the tub, no clothes on, and a man came in and turned on the water. There were two handles, one for cold on the left and one for hot on the right. He only turned on the right one. It took only a few minutes for the heat to get so intense that I almost passed out. The hot water burned my feet, and the pain got worse and worse. I started to scream and cry wanting him to beat me instead of burn me. He finally turned off the water and told me to get out of the tub. I limped all the way over to my bed, climbed in and lay down. The pain was so intense I struggled to breathe. When the man left the room, I crawled over to a box he had left about four feet away from my bed. I ripped the cardboard lid off the box and made little pieces to stick between my toes to keep the skin from sticking together. I put socks on both feet. The next morning when I woke up, I was sweating and my feet hurt so much I could hardly stand it.

Another kid brought me some stuff called *Bag Balm* that was used to heal cracks on the ponies teats. When I pulled my socks off to clean my feet and to put this stuff on them, all the skin came off with the sock. The cardboard was stuck between each one of my toes, but I was able to rip enough of it out to put new cardboard in with the *Bag Balm*. The ointment smelled pretty bad but so did my feet. I was really worried that someone was going to find out that I was trying to take care of them. It took about five or six weeks to walk comfortably again. Forcing my feet into my shoes every morning was an effort all its own.

Over and over I begged God to let it end. Somehow, someway let this torture stop. Make it so they don't hurt me anymore. But it didn't stop. One night after I was finally able to walk again, a man and a woman came to the door and told us all to get dressed that we had somewhere to go. It was dark out, and I wondered what was going to happen to us. Earlier we had heard some kid screaming then all of a sudden, it stopped. The whole place was silent for a few moments. I looked around outside as I was standing there with the rest of the kids. Two counselors were standing in front of us. They took us around the corner of the building and brought us up to these three gunny sacks. I don't know what was in those bags, but they were heavy.

We were told to pick up the bags and that we were going on a hike. When we got to the top of the mountain we were exhausted. I was sweating so badly from carrying that stupid bag all the way up the mountain. We were told to throw the bags down by the tree. Then we turned around and were sent on our way back down that mountain. About fifty feet down this kid in front of me threw a big rock into a pile where there was a bunch of other rocks. When we got to the bottom I asked that kid why he threw that rock into the pile. Nobody but this kid had done that. He said, "Every time I go up there, I throw a rock into that pile to remember that one of us was left up there." I realized then that there was someone in those bags that we had dragged up there. Someone that would be there forever and no one was ever going to know. From that moment on, I was petrified for my life.

I wasn't sure I was going to live long, but I didn't want to die slowly. I wanted it to happen fast or in my sleep. Days slowly dragged by. People came and went. Kids came that I saw briefly, and then they disappeared the next day.

I don't know for sure what happened, but one night I was with another boy. We were walking and walked up to another cabin to see what was in there. A woman was giving a bath to a little girl about two years old. When we walked up to look into the door to see what was going on, the woman looked up and saw us. She then pushed the baby under the water and held her there until the girl stopped moving and bubbles stopped coming up. She jerked the limp baby up by her legs and whipped her across the floor in front of us. She hit a pole and spun around and stopped. Then the woman grabbed both of us and slammed us up against a wall. She told us if we said anything about what we had seen that this would happen to us too. By then I was so paranoid and scared I couldn't even speak. I just sat in shock.

A short time later, the sherriff and an ambulance showed up. I went to tell the sherriff what was really going on in that place, but I was grabbed by two counselors and brought to the tack room. They locked me in there for four or five days with nothing on but my underwear. Bugs were climbing on me. It was cold as hell out there at night, hot as hell during the day. Sometimes I would fall asleep and when I awoke I couldn't remember how many days had passed. I was so thirsty, nowhere to go to the bathroom, no food to eat, nothing. Minutes felt like hours, days like weeks. Nothing to do but lay there thinking of ways I could try to get out of there. Then thinking of all the ways I could die. God wouldn't help me. I kept begging Him, and He kept turning me down. No death. I always woke up the next day to suffer more. All I wanted was to go to school and be loved. Nobody loved me; nobody cared. One safe place to be cared for and loved, that or death is all I wanted.

One time I had been hit so hard by one of the counselors with a piece of wood that it made an egg shaped black and blue mark on my forehead, and it made my eyes turn black. My social worker, Liz, stopped in to check on my progress. She asked me what had happened. I told her I ran in to a pole at the playground. Telling the truth would have gotten me killed. I had been warned not to say anything to anyone about what had happened. I really wasn't interested in dying, but I was interested in a better way of life. Luckily, Liz believed me.

Not only did I dread sunrise and sunset, but I dreaded every moment of my life now. Liz left that day kind of wondering about things. I didn't put anything up front, but that was okay. Collin, one of the "counselors", came to our cabin one day with a pipe about a foot long and a half inch in diameter. I didn't know what it was for, but he made us take off our shoes. Each one of us went into the bedroom and Collin whacked us with that pipe. I thought I was just going to get a beating, but when I told him I was going to run away from there because he was beating us again, he stuck the pipe over my big toe and dislocated it by snapping it sideways. Later on I figured out how to snap my toe back into place. So using the door as a wedge, I managed to snap it back. It hurt so bad, I must have passed out. I don't remember. I woke up in a cold sweat.

Collin came in a couple more times and stuck that pipe inside me, in my rectum. He stuck that pipe down my throat until I gagged and fell unconscious. I pissed and shit my pants when he did that and I got beaten for that too.

Collin and another "counselor" held me down and made me swallow big round pills. I don't know what they were. It was really bad. Half the time I couldn't go to the bathroom, pee or poop. It was terrifying. I remember another time the "counselors" came in and took a leather strap and tied it around my testicles and pulled the strap up behind me. It was so extremely painful that I finally passed out.

These kinds of things went on for about 2 ½ or 3 years. Everyday, every single day, I was angry and scared and hurt. I was never grateful for being alive. I was never grateful for being me. I stopped caring and didn't think anybody out there cared about me either. I dreaded every second of every miserable day. I was numb. Then Liz showed up. She was there to take me home.

Liz said, "I'm here to get you and take you home. Do you want to pack your stuff?" I ran so fast it took me about 3.5 seconds to pack everything I owned and wanted, and I left. I jumped into Liz's car and rolled up the window. She got in and asked if something was wrong. I said, "Nope." She asked, "Aren't you going to say goodbye?" I said, "Yep." I rolled the window down about an inch and yelled goodbye then rolled it right back up. I felt so guilty about all of those kids I was leaving behind, but there was nothing I could do for them. We got a few miles down the road and Liz asked me what was wrong? I said, "I just want to go home and see my mom."

REFLECTIONS OF A MIRACLE

Chapter Four

I wasn't immediately returned to my mom. At first I had to stay with these people called the McNelsons for about three weeks to get used to moving back home. Why, I will never understand, but they were the first people that were ever nice to me. I got to eat everyday, shower everyday and I could lock the door behind me when I went in to the bathroom for a shower or to go to the bathroom. It was a pain free, terror free place. It was wonderful there.

I was by then about fifteen years old. I didn't know anything about anything. I mean about how things worked in the world – NOTHING. My Mom was living at 1695 Patterson Lane, Santa Cruz, California. She was not with my step-father any longer. I knew nothing of what had happened with my mom and my brothers and sister after my stepfather had been arrested, and I knew nothing of what had happened to him since his arrest. I found out about three years later that he had gotten just a six month sentence for molestation. He was on work release during the day and returned to jail at night. I had spent more time in "prison" than he had.

Isn't that a slap in the face. The victim does more time than the sex offender does. There is something seriously wrong with that. I still suffer from nightmares of him sexually assaulting me. I also still have nightmares about my father beating me repeatedly. I tried to go back to public school, I really tried, but I had missed so much that I felt like I didn't fit in. You know, like the kid with the dunce hat in the corner on the stool. I felt like that dumb kid all the time.

At fifteen years of age I couldn't even tell you the whole alphabet. I was dyslexic and couldn't read or write, however, I could spell Tony. It became a daily event for me to be sent to the principal's office. I couldn't learn so I would get mad and yell at the teachers or the kid next to me for not helping me to understand. I felt so out of place. Other kids could read, and I couldn't. It was so frustrating for me so I lashed out. Eventually they put me on a work release program. All I had to do was show up at school, sign my name and leave. The great California educational system can't teach them so send them out to the wolves.

Three months later I just stopped going in altogether. They did nothing about it. My mother moved us to Clearlake, California, where we lived for about six months. I tried again to go back to school there at Lower Lake High School. Didn't work. I got sick at school one day with flu-like symptoms and my buddy wanted to drive my car home. I said okay and we got in. We pulled out and got on the main road to town.

My car had a 440 police interceptor motor. When it was pushed over the limits it was super fast. My buddy asked if he could punch it? I said yeah, go. He punched it and the throttle stuck. The car was running wide open. When he tried to stop it, there was a school bus in front of us. We swerved, hit the guard rail and flipped over. The roofs of the vehicles touched as we flipped over the top of the bus. We landed on a bridge and a Mercedes Benz hit us broad side at full speed. We started rolling, side over side. I flew through the windshield and landed on the next bridge down. I was knocked unconscious.

When I came to I could hear people talking. I felt the warmth of the road on my face. I knew I was still alive, but I couldn't feel anything. I couldn't see because my eyes were covered with blood. I heard a voice say, "You have been in an accident, don't move." Someone wiped the blood out of my eyes and I saw a shiny badge and a smiling face. It was a fireman.

I didn't know it at the time, but I had a massive skull fracture, a broken jaw and had ground half of my face off skidding on the pavement. All of my bottom teeth were folded back in my mouth from the impact. I had severe lacerations to my tongue, my jaw, skull and other assorted areas. I had broken my pelvis. My right foot was at the top of my head next to my left shoulder. I was rushed to the hospital not expected to make it. Doctors came in to the emergency room and told my mom they couldn't help me. They heavily medicated me for a 2 ½ hour ride in an ambulance to Santa Rosa Trauma Center where the doctors put me back together. I was hospitalized for three months. When I was released, I went back to the school and found out that they all thought I had died. After I recovered we moved down to Santa Cruz.

I met a guy in Santa Cruz and started working on cars. That didn't last because I really knew nothing about cars. My brothers came over one night and asked if I wanted to go roller skating?

I said, "Sure." I had never been roller skating before. I put those roller skates on and gave it a whirl. I was the falling fool out there until I finally got the hang of it. I skated around once and this really pretty girl skated by me. She had on white pants that wrapped around her legs and tied in front. They were cool and she was beautiful. I learned her name was Brook. She was about my age. I had just turned sixteen.

My brothers had brought a bottle of Bacardi 151. They told me to go ask Brook if she and her friend wanted to come with us. They agreed. We went to a park and had some Bacardi. It tasted like gasoline to me, but Brook must have liked it and drank quite a bit. I didn't know what alcohol could do to a person. I had never seen a girl naked before and thought this was my big chance. I took Brook behind a tree in the park. I got her shirt up and her pants halfway down when my brother turned on the head lights of the car and she put her clothes back on really fast.

We got back in the car and drove to San Jose to Jamie's house. Jamie was my brother's friend. Jamie took one of the girls into a room and Brook and I went into the other room. She kissed me for the first time, and I put my hand inside her shirt. I had no clue what I was doing. I didn't know what the hell that thing was she was wearing underneath her shirt, but she kindly helped me get it off.

This was the first time I ever had sex with a woman. I can't say it was love, but after we were done I asked Brook to marry me. She said, "Yes." It sounded good at the time. She had made me feel wanted in a way I had never felt before, so we began dating. Now she was all mine.

About a month later Brook came over to see me. She told me she was pregnant and I said that was nice. Of course I had no clue what that meant. She asked me if I knew what that was? I said, "No." When she told me I was the baby's father I started yelling, "How did you let this happen?" It was all her fault. I remembered hearing a friend say, "If you play, you will pay." I guess I had had all the fun I was going to have.

Brook moved in to a motel with me and now I had to figure out how to take care of her and me and a baby when it got here. SCARY. I had never had a job before, and I had no education to help me get one. We had to do all kinds of crazy things to survive. I mowed lawns for $5. I had to make $21 a day for the motel room. Anything above that was for food and gas for the lawnmower.

One day my sister came by and said Mom was sick and we needed to go to Oregon to see her. My mom had moved back in with my step-father. So we all went to Oregon. My mom told us she was dying. She had cancer. That was why she had gone back to my step-dad. She needed someone to take care of her. Not a one of us could help her since we were all just barely getting by. Mom was going through chemo but was losing her battle with cancer. It was just a matter of time before I lost her again, this time for good.

Mom looked at my girlfriend and said, "You're pregnant, aren't you?" Brook answered, "Yes." Mom said she was glad because the baby would give her a reason to hang on. We left Oregon to return home to Santa Cruz where Brook finally gave birth. We were on welfare at the time so the birth was covered. We had a son and named him Antonio after me. I hoped Antonio wasn't going to be a loser like me. I didn't know how to read or write, so how was I going to provide for this little life? I kept trying job after job after job, anything I could do just to get by. I called Mom and told her I had a baby, no money, and I didn't know what to do. Mom told us to come to Oregon that she would send us bus tickets. I told her we would drive and we did.

We stayed in a small house for about two months. I saw my mom on and off as she went in and out of the hospital. During that time I went to the police twice and told them about the way my step-dad was treating my girlfriend and baby while my mom was in the hospital. He was threatening us, yelling at Brook, taking our baby and hiding him. He was trying to make us move away. I had to be around this person I hated so much just to be with my mom for the little time I got to spend with her. I loved mom so much.

Brook and I married in my mom's living room. I was trying to give mom comfort that I was going to be okay after she was gone. I didn't want her to worry about me. Mom was getting weaker and weaker as the days went by. She had lost all of her hair and was so thin. She still managed to smile every time she held her new grandson.

Dealing with my step dad finally became too much so we moved back down to California. We said goodbye to my mom. That would be the last time I would see her alive.

My new wife and I were having a really hard time. I couldn't keep a job, and we were struggling. So we packed up and moved to Andover, Minnesota, where my father lived. I thought I could make things right with this man who had beaten me all the time and seemed to have no conscience. I had a family of my own now so surely things could be different.

My little family and I stayed with my father and my stepmother for a couple of months. During that time my stepmother showed her true colors. She was as wicked and evil as ever. She was always fighting with my dad about us being there. She told my dad that she would leave if we didn't. She said we weren't her children. She had said the same thing in a letter to my dad years ago when she threatened to kill herself if he didn't get rid of us. My dad showed me the letter years later after they had divorced.

Anthony Mucciaccaro

I moved my wife and son to Anoka, Lincoln Estates, Apartment 210. We were still on welfare. Things were rough, very rough. My wife had a diaphragm so she wouldn't get pregnant. We know now those things aren't always foolproof. After a night of fighting, we made up and had sex. A diaphragm has to stay in for a certain length of time after sex for it to work, however, Brook took it out that morning right after we had sex. At nineteen years of age Brook was pregnant again. The baby was due in October.

REFLECTIONS OF A MIRACLE

Anthony Mucciaccaro

Chapter Five

It was the middle of September when I got the worst call of my life. My stepfather called and said, "If you want to see your mother alive, you better come now," and hung up. I flew to California, picked up my younger brother and we started driving to Oregon. Along the way my brother and I talked about the good times we had had with her. We laughed a lot. The trip was long so we drove all night. When the sun began to rise my brother looked at me and said, "She's dead." He felt it. We both started crying and drove faster hoping we were wrong.

When we got to the house, we raced down the driveway and got out of the car. The front door opened and there he stood. I will never forget it. All my step-dad said was, "Your mother is in the morgue." He turned around and shut the door.

My older brother was at the breaking point. I was so angry that mom had spent her final moments with this evil asshole who had taken more from our family than the cancer that had killed our mom. My older brother wanted to even the score. We had to talk him out of shooting my step-dad. We didn't want him to take anything else from us. It was over now and there was nothing that would bring mom back.

Our aunt showed up, our mom's identical twin. She got us a motel room so we could clean up and eat. The next day was the funeral. We all went. I stood in the back until everyone had left. Mom was lying in the casket on the other side of the room. I forced myself to walk over. I couldn't say goodbye. I didn't want to lose her again. I just stood there screaming and yelling asking her why she had let this happen to me? Why had she brought me into a world that was so cruel, mean and vicious, so terrifying? I had gone through so much torture and she ended up dying on me just when I needed her most. How could she do such a thing? My screaming and yelling did me no good. She was gone. I left and didn't go to the burial. A part of me died that day, too. At the request of my step-dad, we all went back to his house. We sat down at this big table. My step-dad was at the end of the table when he took out my mom's will.

In so many words he told us that there was nothing for us.

Together they had hundreds of thousands of dollars in property and bank accounts, but he couldn't even put us up in a motel or fly us home. In fact, to this day there is no stone to mark her grave. I have never been to her grave, but someday I will go there and mark it for all of us.

If my step-dad burns in hell for eternity, it still won't be enough. I went back to Santa Cruz and got a flight back to Minnesota.

My daughter was born in October and for the next 3 months or so my wife and I fought almost constantly. We finally decided to call it quits, and Brook flew back to California with the kids. I went back to California a short time later and we were divorced. I tried to see my kids for visitation, but if I was ever even one minute late it was a fight. Brook wouldn't let me see them or take them. This went on for about a month and a half before she finally asked me to leave and never come back. So I did. That is something I still regret doing, but hind-sight is 20/20.

I moved to Albuquerque, New Mexico, to live with my sister. Two weeks later my sister moved out, and I had nowhere to live. I met a girl and moved in with her. We had a stormy relationship.

At one time during the three years I lived in New Mexico, I drove up to Minnesota to see if I could work things out with my dad, but to no avail. We just didn't mesh so I went back to New Mexico and

REFLECTIONS OF A MIRACLE

tried again with that girl, but that didn't work either. I couldn't keep it together and couldn't hold a job.

After a year I decided to move north again. I went back to Minnesota and moved into a basement room. I stayed there for a while and met another girl. We had been dating for a very short time when she came to me and said she was pregnant. We went to tell her mom and dad. Her dad freaked out and I ran for the door, but her mom made it there first. They were upset, but mostly concerned.

I still couldn't hold a job. Things were frustrating to me. If people were too nice I wondered what they wanted from me. A lot of fights happened between Michele and me and between her parents and me because I misunderstood things all the time.

Michele and I had a little boy in February, 1990. We got married after he was born. That marriage lasted about a year and a half. It wasn't her fault. I just didn't fit in with anybody. I moved further north, further away from people, thinking that would help.

Chapter Six

I moved to a little town called St. Francis, Minnesota. I found a job listed in the newspaper for a maintenance man at an apartment complex. I was a real talker, so I talked my way into that job. I could fix anything if I could see something just like it already working.

One day the fire alarms went off. I didn't know what to do so I called 9-1-1. The fire department showed up and turned the alarm off. They told me that the fire marshal would come by and show me how to operate the alarm system. He came hours later and show me how to operate the system.

In our conversation I asked him how someone could become a fireman? He said to become a firefighter you had to have a high school diploma or a GED, fill out an application with the city and be willing to lay it on the line. I said, "I've got a high school diploma and I'm willing to lay it on the line." So the next day I went to the city and filled out an application.

I was called before the city council. A council member asked me why I wanted to become a firefighter? Before I knew it I answered what my heart felt. "I want to help people," I said. "In their worst moments, I want to help them."

They hired me on the spot. I was a volunteer fireman. WOW. I am the dumbest, with no schooling, no skills, no vocabulary, but I had a big heart. I thought I could really be somebody now. I went to the fire station immediately I was so excited. I met the chief. He shook my hand and then gave me all my gear- jacket, turn out pants, helmet, gloves, safety belt and boots. I was also given a fire pager. The chief told me I could be in the trucks and run calls, but I had to go to fire fighter school and EMS training before I could be a full-fledged fire fighter. I had two years to complete my schooling. Isn't it funny, I was more scared of the school part than I was of putting my life on the line for a perfect stranger.

A couple of days went by, and I decided to go and see this big town of St. Francis. I stopped at a little strip mall that had a video store in it. I had this kid with me that helped me out at the apartments, so we went in to get a video. We walked in and I saw this girl behind the counter. She was absolutely beautiful. God had blessed me with a vision. I asked, "Is this the liquor store?"

She simply replied, "No."

I turned and whacked the kid with me and said, "I told you this wasn't the liquor store," and we walked out. Then I walked back in. That didn't get her attention though, so I rented four or five movies. I was trying to figure out how to talk to her, but she wasn't cooperating so I signed my name Mickey Mouse on the slip. That didn't work either.

I kept the movies past the return date hoping she would call me to tell me they were late. She never did. I didn't make very much money so I thought I better take them back. I walked in the door and she was there. She said, "Well if it isn't Mickey Mouse." She was standing there with her friend so I went over and asked her why she hadn't called me. "That isn't my job," she said. I had kept those movies for no reason. The three of us talked a while. I asked her if she was married and she said no. I was sliding her quarters and asking her to call me- writing it on Post-It notes and sliding it to her. She walked over to the computer, pulled up my account and went to the phone and dialed my number. She left a message on my answering machine. "There, I called you. Are you happy now? Bye," she said and hung up. Right in front of me she did that and I just about passed out. I couldn't believe it. I was in love with her the second she did that. I wanted her in my world no matter what.

REFLECTIONS OF A MIRACLE

I turned to leave. On my way out the door, I gave her the "call me" sign. When I got home I listened to the answering machine so many times I thought I would break the tape. Then the phone rang and it was her. We talked for a while on the phone then I asked her to come over. She asked me the dumbest question I had ever heard from a beautiful woman, "If I come over there, can I trust you to be good?"

I said, "Honey, I'll be anything you want, just come over." I even offered to pay her $10 an hour to clean my apartment and do laundry just to get her to come over. She did.

We talked from 9:30 PM until 1:00 AM. It was snowing out, and I convinced Kay, who had lived in Minnesota her whole life and had probably driven in ten inches of snow before, that it was too dangerous to drive home in the 1/8 inch of snow that had fallen. She said okay because she was tired.

I gave her sweat pants and a tee shirt to wear. We lay down on my super single bed. I put my hand on her hip and we cuddled up really close. I moved my hand from her hip to her belly and she said, "Your losing trust," so I moved that hand right back to her hip. I don't think either of us got any sleep that night. I had a lot of respect for that lady.

The next morning we got up and dressed. I gave her a key to my house and she said she would come by later. I paid her $80 for doing eight hours worth of laundry the next week. It took two months before she finally came by and never left.

We lived together at the apartments for about three months when I decided to go over the road truck driving, and I wanted Kay to go with me. I found a company that would let me take her with me. I drove and she was my navigator and log book writer. She could read and write. What a team we made. I didn't know it then, but because of the fear inside me and the will to be the best I could be, it was hard for me to be calm. I didn't want anything to happen to her. All I knew how to do was drive. I had to rely on someone to help me with directions and paper work and Kay was it. Driving together was fun. We had good times. I drove for three months and then we decided to start a Bobcat business with her sister and brother-in-law.

We lived in the basement of their home. We lived there for five months and then moved out. With a little help from her mom and dad we bought out her sister and brother-in law and changed the business's name.

I started fire fighter school and was running the business, too. Kay read those books to me and

REFLECTIONS OF A MIRACLE

helped me pass firefighter I and II at Anoka Technical College. I passed those college courses by memorizing everything. I then took and passed the first responder course. When you dialed 9-1-1 – It was me who showed up. Then I passed a state medical test and got a license as a medical first responder.

There was nothing I couldn't do with that woman by my side. I was on top of the world. The fire department made me a real person. I was somebody. I was proud to have achieved what everyone said I couldn't do. I held three certificates and would go on to collect 32 in all including becoming an instructor of auto extraction during my seven years with the fire department.

I remember my first fire call. It was 2:00 AM in the morning when my pager went off. We had just set up a huge water bed in our room and hadn't finished moving the other furniture around, so when I jumped from the bed, I hit the wall then turned and ran into the dresser. I was determined to make it out the door. I went to the living room, grabbed a pair of pants and a tee shirt off the back of the couch and out the door I went. I drove to the fire department as fast as I could, got my gear on and went to the call in Engine One. There seemed to be something in my boots. I thought it might be some kind of hazing by the other firefighters. When we got to the house, fire was shooting out the windows. I ran around the house with a one and a half inch hose line when a car on fire rolled out of the garage all by itself. The wiring had melted together, the car was in gear and it sparked the starter. I started putting water on what was left of the garage and another firefighter came up to help me. The hose jerked out of my hands and hit my face mask, knocking it loose. I sucked in a lot of smoke. I couldn't stop coughing so I went to the ambulance and asked for oxygen. They insisted on taking me to the hospital for smoke inhalation.

When we got to the emergency room, they took off my jacket then my boots. When they pulled off my turn-out pants, the nurse lifted my leg and to my surprise I saw I was wearing my girlfriend's stirrup pants. I had mistakenly put on Kay's pants in the dark getting dressed. It took me three months to live that down. My first fire and I wore my girlfriend's stirrup pants. How embarrassing.

I remember my first medical call. It came over as difficulty breathing. An elderly man was having chest pains and difficulty breathing. He was having a heart attack. When we arrived I quickly did a primary survey – blood pressure, pulse and respiration. I started him on oxygen wide open. When the ambulance arrived, it was a load and go situation. When the victim reached the hospital he was immediately taken in for a triple bypass.

REFLECTIONS OF A MIRACLE

A few weeks later I saw the man in town with his wife. He wasn't moving too fast. I went up and said hi and asked how he was doing. He was absolutely overwhelmed with gratitude. He kept saying that I had saved his life. It shocked me to realize that I had been a part of actually saving someone's life.

From that moment on, every time my pager went off, it was a race to help that next person or save that next house. The adrenalin rush was so intense. I tried to be the best fire fighter I could be.

I became a fire motor operator and ran the rescue squad. Calls were the number one thing to me. Once, there was a personal injury accident with two cars involved. Two victims had been ejected from their vehicle. When we arrived on the scene I grabbed the med kit and ran to the victim lying in the ditch. The other firefighter went to the second vehicle. Rescue II was in route. My victim was a little girl about seven or eight years old. I told her my name and that I was there to help her. I wanted her to relax, tell me where she hurt. Another fire fighter ran up and held c-spine to immobilize her. I told the little girl not to move her head. She said her legs hurt and her belly hurt. I did a primary survey starting with her legs. Both were broken. As I moved up to her belly, I opened her heavy winter jacket. There was a four inch piece of steel protruding from her lower abdomen. I now had a critical victim on my hands.

There was another victim laying about twelve feet away that other firefighters were working on. I leaned back and used my radio to notify 2800 to launch Life Link. If we airlifted the victim, the trip to the hospital would be approximately ten minutes. I leaned back to the little girl and told her I had a special ride coming for her. Another firefighter brought over splints for her legs and a long board. We could hear Life Link coming.

The little girl started crying and asking for her mother who had been driving the car. I looked over to the firefighters. One looked back and shook his head back and forth. Her mom didn't make it. I told the little girl that I was helping her and that the others would help her mom.

We rolled her to her side to put the long board under her. We didn't notice in time that she could see her mother's boots sticking out from under a sheet. When we rolled her back, she was very upset. The helicopter landing was very noisy. The girl asked me if her mom had died? I felt so bad, but I told her the truth. We loaded her on the helicopter. When I reached in to put the seat belt on her, she grabbed my arm and said, "Thank you." I told her it

REFLECTIONS OF A MIRACLE

was my job. She said, "No, thank you for telling me the truth."

After undergoing surgery and an extended stay in the hospital, the little girl made a full recovery. Those are some of the things that firefighters deal with everyday of their life. It's not just putting water on a fire, it's laying your life on the line to save someone else's life. I loved being a firefighter.

Chapter Seven

I married my girlfriend, Kay, a year and a half after I met her. I had the fire department chief, assistant chief, lieutenant and my older brother as my best man and groomsmen. I married her on an island at a golf course in Ham Lake, Minnesota. It was a beautiful wedding and the best thing I ever did. When my bride stepped out of that car, I almost passed out she was so stunning.

We were married two years when we decided to start our family. We got pregnant and this time it was something we both wanted. Life was good, but underneath the surface something wasn't quite right with me; something in my head was going wrong. I just didn't know what.

My wife went into premature labor at 32 weeks. I remember her telling a story of the nurse practioner. The nurse asked Kay if she was having contractions and Kay saying, "How do I know? I've never done this before."

Kay and I had a code that if she needed me, she would call my pager and put in 9-1-1. That meant for me to call right away. I called to find out that she was in Coon Rapids hospital.

Kay was told that she had dilated to 3cm. They were not equipped at Coon Rapids to take a baby at 32 weeks so they were going to take her by ambulance to Abbot Northwestern hospital. I got there just as they were wheeling her out to the ambulance. I said, "I'm riding with her, but the nurse said that I couldn't.

The paramedics knew me from the fire department and said I could go with my wife in my usual seat. Kay was in the hospital for two weeks. They did an amniocentesis on June 10th and on June 12, 1996, our daughter was born 5½ weeks prematurely. She weighed 6 lbs 9 oz and did well on her own. Mother and baby came home three days later.

I was not sure if my wife was ready for a baby since she was only twenty-three, but I was wrong. The mother instinct does exist. Motherhood was a breeze for her. Life was really good now. I had the fire department job, a business and Kay managed the apartment complex. Kay was my fixer. No matter what it was, I looked to her to fix it. She took care of me. No one had ever taken care of me before, and I loved her more and more everyday. I could never thank her enough for all that she did.

Anthony Mucciaccaro

I could never show or tell her how much I really appreciated her. I always kissed her goodbye every time I went out the door for a fire call just in case anything ever happened to me, she would know how much I loved her.

REFLECTIONS OF A MIRACLE

Chapter Eight

Then came the day that would start my downward spiral to losing everything. Tones went off for a grass fire. I arrived at the station and was putting on my gear when the lieutenant told me to go and size up the fire.

Another firefighter and I arrived on the scene of a 15 acre grass fire that was threatening sixteen or seventeen homes. I called back to the lieutenant and told him the size of the fire and what we would need. I turned on my radio and asked 2800 to notify all surrounding departments for mutual aid. I asked them to notify DNR for additional equipment. We turned on sprinklers at the houses throwing them on the roofs, anything we could do to stop the fire from spreading. We ran from house to house then started the attack on the fire. The wind shifted and the fire came at us at rapid speed. I had on full turnout gear and five gallons of water on my back. It was already a hot day so when I tried to run from the fire, I was over taken with heat and down I went.

All I remember was the feeling of someone dragging me and water hitting me. I woke up in an am-

REFLECTIONS OF A MIRACLE

bulance in my underwear. The paramedic said I had heat stroke.

My wife had my pager at home and had heard what was going on. She got someone to watch our daughter and headed for the fire station. When they told her it was me, she demanded to know if I was all right. She told them they had better get on that radio and let her talk to me or she was going to the fire scene to find out for herself. They did exactly what she wanted. I talked to her and told her I was okay and was going to stay at the fire. She insisted that I come home, so I did.

Now what I am about to tell you I kept under wraps for a year and a half. I began having feelings that someone was coming to get me again; I was going to be hurt, raped, murdered or something was going to happen to my family. I couldn't sleep. I was having bad dreams of things I hadn't thought about in years. So, of course, I went to my wife for her to "fix it." She listened to me one night and said I needed to go and get help that this was something she couldn't "fix". She said, "I know you want me to, but I don't know how to fix this."

The next day I called a psychologist I found in the phone book and made an appointment. I told the psychologist how I felt and she asked if I had ever had anything traumatic happen to me in my life? I just looked at her and answered, "Uh, yeah."

I explained a little about my life, and she told me I had Post Traumatic Stress Disorder and it was probably triggered by the near death experience I had had when I went down in that grass fire. She related PTSD to a Vietnam veteran, putting up a wall to block out traumatic things that had happened around them or to them. Years later something could trigger the memory and that wall disappeared and everything that was locked up in there flooded forward and became real again.

I then went to a psychiatrist who gave me medication to help with the anxiety and depression that was keeping me from sleeping. About a month later I called the doctor and told him the medication wasn't working and he told me to take more, so I did. Pretty soon I stopped calling the doctor and just kept taking more and more. When I had to see the doctor I told him the medication was working.

I kept needing more and more medication. The more I took, the more I needed. I was taking Prozac and Soma. When my wife figured out I was popping the Soma like candy, the doctor switched me to Clonazapam which was a form of Valium. The Prozac was switched to Zoloft. I began to grind my teeth and felt very aggressive on Zoloft so I went back to Prozac. To help me sleep, they added Zyprexa, an anti-psychotic drug.

My wife read, "The Pill Book," to see what the pills were for. That worked for a while. I was taking my meds, smoking pot, plus taking "mini whites" – basically legal speed. I began taking another drug that would turn out to be crank to keep me awake for days at a time so I could run a snow plow. On all those drugs I went from 135 lbs to 235 in one month! No joke, one month. All I could think about was how to get high, how to numb the pain of the memories and nightmares that flooded my days and nights. I no longer lived, I survived. I constantly fought with my wife.

When I did anything I thought I had to give 110% and then 15% more just to keep up with the rest of the world. So when it came to doing the drugs to numb the pain, I went overboard. It just kept snowballing.

One day my wife looked at me and saw that my eyes, hands, and face were puffy. A little while later I ended up in the hospital. I had over-dosed! I said it was an accident when they asked me what had happened. I just could not escape far enough. The second I started to feel the medication wearing off, the paranoia, the looking over my shoulder, the scared feeling that someone was coming to get me or my family would return. I often drove around higher than a kite and talked to people who would later call my wife and ask her if I had been drinking. She told them no, but when I got back to the house she was not happy about the phone calls.

My wife wanted me to go to the hospital but I told her she didn't know what she was talking about. I asked her where the girls were. She said they were right there and pointed to them sitting watching TV in the living room. I was at the kitchen table; she was in the kitchen. Then I asked her, "Who is that?" and pointed down the hallway towards our daughters' bedroom.

She looked and said, "Who? Where?"

I pointed again. She looked at me and said, "There is nothing there. You are seeing things." I just blew it off, but we continued to argue about my going to the hospital.

Kay called my brother. When he showed up he said either I was going to the hospital or he was calling 9-1-1. I told my wife that if they kept me in the hospital one night, I would kill her. She simply told me that I could ride to the hospital with my brother. I said I would ride with her but my brother said, "No, you're riding with me."

I asked, "Why?" and he said, "You just threatened to kill your wife so let's go, big guy." I rode with my brother. When we arrived, I had nothing but dagger looks for my wife. I even told her that she wouldn't be going back with me to talk to the doctors. She said that was fine that she would send my brother with me and he would tell them the truth. I wasn't happy about that either. I was so far gone that I had actually threatened to kill the one person I loved and trusted the most. The crazy part is that at the time I meant it. I was that messed up.

I remember bits and pieces of my stay in the hospital. I don't know how much time had gone went when a lady and a doctor came into my room. They wanted to help me with some kind of rehabilitation. All those bad thoughts and feelings were back. Nobody, except maybe another addict, knows how I felt. I thought I could get high to kill the pain inside.

I was taken to a locked rehab ward. One or two nights of that and some freaky things, whether they were in my head or not, and I wanted out so I could get high. My legs hurt so bad from the muscles tighting up. It got to the point that I thought I was really going to die. Everything in my head was rushing. I couldn't control my emotions. All I could think of was getting out.

I called my wife and begged her to get me out. I promised I would never abuse my meds again that she could give them to me, lock them up, whatever made her comfortable.

My wife came to get me out. I had voluntarily gone in, so they couldn't stop her from taking me out. The saying goes that you always hurt the ones you love. That's just a way to justify all the wrong things you do just so you will feel better.

The second we got home from rehab, my wife locked up my pills. For a while I stuck with exactly what I was suppose to take. I was helping create a false sense of security for her. She was counting my pills daily, maybe even more times than I knew. Eventually she was trusting enough that she stopped counting them. She felt things were going okay and that's when I gained more trust and more access to the pills.

"Lies" is a small word, but it can destroy any and everything. Lies come easily and quickly, but it can take a lifetime to fix the damage done by those lies. We were apartment managers and my wife had to leave to check on one of the apartments. When she left I opened that lockbox so fast and I took as many pills as I could before she got back.

REFLECTIONS OF A MIRACLE

Most people think rationally. I never thought that way. All I could think of was how, where and when I could get high and stay there. Nothing else mattered. Not even the most important things in my life, my wife, my children, friends or my life.

When you're high and numb, nothing else matters. You feel NOTHING. One way I used to look at it was I was already dead because I surely did not feel anything.

In early 2001 my wife and I filed for bankruptcy on our company. Our business had fallen apart and I had lost my job as a volunteer firemen. I could no longer do the job, and it was upsetting everybody. I actually had my wife join the fire department so she could be my witness. It was always someone else's fault, not mine. I was arguing about calls, swearing at people, telling them they were wrong. I couldn't control myself. During the time I was with the fire department it was great, but when it ended, it ended badly. It hurt really bad to leave because I loved it so much. Things just went down hill faster after that.

Chapter Nine

We moved to Monticello, MN, and things started down the same path again. My wife was doing it all. She was running three apartment complexes in two cities. As things got worse with my drug use and my excuses, she did almost everything at the apartments. What she couldn't do she would find someone to do it.

I found new doctors, but this time I told them about the overdoses thinking maybe it wouldn't happen again. Yeah, right! Things got worse. I started telling my wife that my back hurt. I was huge so how would she know if my back really hurt or not. I was going to the hospital telling them my back hurt and they always came though.

They gave me prescriptions and shots and my wife didn't even know I was filling the prescriptions. I would fill them, dump the bottles then go back to the pharmacy with a story that my kids had put them down the toilet or I had dropped them down the sink and I needed them refilled and they always did it.

I went from hospital to hospital on the same day for shots and prescriptions. I got so bad that I actually timed my wife when she got up to go to the bathroom. In the amount of time she was gone, I could get up, take a handful of pills and be back in my same spot before she got back. She never knew that's how bad my addiction was.

My sister-in-law came to the house one day to see my wife. When she walked in the door she couldn't believe what I looked like. My entire body was swollen. Everywhere. I had overdosed again. I had no idea I was so high. She took my children with her and left. My wife dialed 9-1-1.

Into an ambulance I went again. This was not going to be good. I had broken a promise to my wife again. I had gotten non-narcotic pills for anxiety and overdosed on them. My wife called the psychiatrist's office where I had gotten the pills. His secretary answered and my wife asked to speak to the doctor. The lady told her the doctor was unavailable at the moment but would call her back. My wife wasn't having that so she said, "Look, I need to talk to him now. Later may be too late." The lady asked my wife what the problem was. When she told her, the lady on the phone tried to sympathize with her.

My wife asked her, "Are you a drug addict?" The reply was, no. "Are you married to a drug addict?"

Again the reply was, no. "Then you don't know how I feel or what battles I have had just so my husband won't drive around messed up like that with my children in the car, so get me the doctor now." She did.

When the doctor got on the phone, my wife explained the problem again in great detail. I was overtaking the non narcotic pills and she asked what the doctor was thinking giving me more. He said, "Well, all I can do is prescribe the medications and hope that he takes them like he is suppose to. I can't watch him 24/7."

My wife replied, "Neither can I. Remember this conversation when he's dead and I'm suing you for his death," and she hung up.

My children watched their daddy fall apart little by little. My wife watched, the only person who ever truly loved me in this cruel world watched as I fell apart, helplessly. No matter what she did or said, it was too late to stop. I had torn everything apart. This woman had been blissfully in love with me and I had repaid her by giving her nothing but heartache and pain. I would pass out with lit cigarettes in my hand, burn holes in my robe or clothes. I would leave long burn marks on the kitchen table. My wife was afraid to go to sleep. She would take my lighters and hide them so she could sleep, and what would

I do? Wait for her to go to sleep and then I'd run to the hospital in the middle of the night for a shot of anything I could get.

It wasn't long before my wife finally hit her breaking point. She and I went into our bedroom. She turned, and looked at me and said I had wrecked everything, it was over. She no longer wanted to be with me or take care of me. There was nothing left in our lives. The apartments were selling and the owners could not find anything else to buy. Kay wanted me to leave and get away from her and the children. I was hurting them all. She had a family and responsibilities and she had suffered long enough. She couldn't watch me destroy everything anymore. Kay's only choice was to get rid of the danger in the children's life. She had to protect them and since the danger was me, I needed to leave.

It took two months for a final split. She had been living down stairs in another apartment but finally moved home to her parents. I didn't want to live. I hated every moment I was alive because of the loss of my family. All my life I had struggled to be a human being and to be respected and to make something of my life. I had lost everything. Now I had no direction in my life, nothing to hang on to anymore.

I had learned respect and honesty from my wife, but I destroyed it all. I lied to her to cover up the pain of all the things that had happened to me before she was ever there. Life wasn't fun anymore. I was scared and alone. There was only one thing left to do, end it all. I made that decision and refilled all of my medications.

I called my wife and told her to call me at 10:00 PM that night. I dropped my son off at his mom's house and left all my fire things with him – pictures, certificates, plaques, everything. I drove to the hospital parking lot because I didn't want just anyone to find my body and be messed up because of it. At least at the hospital they had seen that kind of thing before. I had spent most of the day wondering if I was doing the right thing and all I could think was, it was the only thing left to do. I had run out of options. There was only emptiness. No more love, no more happiness, no more future. It was all gone.

I dreaded the next morning. I didn't want to see it. I sat there in the hospital parking lot for about forty minutes waiting for 10:00 PM to come.

At that time my phone could only receive incoming phone calls. My wife had restricted my phone because I had run the bill up to over $800 and couldn't pay for it. She called.

I told her I had "fixed" it and everything was going to be all right. I told her it was my turn to take care

REFLECTIONS OF A MIRACLE

of her and the girls and that was what I was going to do. She was in survival mode now trying to take care and support the girls without me.

I had peeled all the labels off the medicine bottles so nobody could tell what I had taken. I took the first handful of pills at five minutes after 10:00 and drank some Dr. Pepper. I talked to my wife a little while longer. I told her I loved her and I cared about her and the girls. I asked her to tell them that their daddy was a great man, that I was a hero once. Tell them that I was sick, and it had overtaken me. Tell them I love them more than anything in the world. I was empty. I was writing a note to my children to say goodbye. I had pictures of us laying on the truck seat so when they found me, they would know who I was in love with and who I was giving my life for.

I had taken two bottles of 60 tablets each of Valium, two bottles of 60 tablets each of Vicodin, one bottle of 145 tablets of Wellbutrin, one bottle of 175 tablets of Depakote and one bottle of 60 tablets of Percocet. I took them all. It took four mouthfuls to finish them all.

I should not even be here telling my story, but thank God I am. I had gone to therapists for six years and nothing had helped. I lay my head back on the seat and waited for the medication to take affect. I knew that I had taken such a massive dosage that I would pass away from it. My system couldn't survive that amount. Being medically qualified I knew I had taken well over the amount needed to kill me. So I relaxed, waiting for the moment to come when I would go to sleep and never wake up again. The pain and suffering would finally end. All I felt was peace and love for my children. They would no longer suffer for their father, my wife would no longer suffer for the love she had lost. There would be no more wrecking their lives, no more pain, no more pressure. It would be over in a flash. They would only have to say goodbye and bury me. Then they could get on with their lives. I was through dragging them down.

REFLECTIONS OF A MIRACLE

Chapter Ten

I realized that there were head lights in front of my truck. It was hospital security. I call him my angel now. He scared me by coming in my direction. I thought that he might call for help, so I backed my truck up, turned and pulled out of the driveway.

Like a brick all that medication I had taken hit me all at once. I had no control left. My jaw locked, my fingers twisted up, I could barely see, my feet couldn't feel the pressure on the pedals. I tried to turn the truck around to go back to the hospital but ended up going across someone's lawn, missing cars and banging off curbs. I came to a stop sign and realized that I couldn't stop. When I did manage to stop, it was too late. I had moved too far into the intersection and a car had scraped the whole front of my truck.

A deputy was right there at the intersection and saw the whole thing. He flipped on his lights. I was unable to walk when I got out of my truck. I fell to the ground several times as I walked along the side of my truck. The medication was affecting me more and more. I could barely speak. The officer asked me if I had been drinking? I said, "No", but he gave

REFLECTIONS OF A MIRACLE

me a breathalyser test. It proved zero three times in a row. The officer asked me to breath harder and I tried. He couldn't figure out what was wrong.

I told him that I had taken too much medication and that I would be fine. He called a tow truck, wrote me an inattentive driving ticket and put me in the tow truck. The tow truck driver dropped me and my truck off at my sister's apartment, handed me my keys and left. I fell all over my sister's apartment breaking things and falling on to the floor. I don't remember how much time passed, but somehow I was back in my truck driving again.

I had to get to the hospital. I wasn't dying fast enough and I started to get scared. I didn't want to be in a position where I would be in a coma for the rest of my life. That's not how I wanted my kids to remember me. I figured I better get help.

When I got on Highway 25 going toward Buffalo, I realized I was on the wrong side of the road. I was going south in the northbound lane. Someone must have called the police because there was a deputy waiting for me. I was so messed up that I drove past the cop and past the turn. I drove right into a ditch just past the hospital. The cops were right behind me.

When I got out of my truck, I fell down several more times and kept trying to get up. I was so far into overdose now that things were uncontrollable; things were flying crazily around me. I couldn't concentrate, couldn't answer questions. All I knew was that I needed help immediately. Right then I heard sirens but couldn't understand where they were coming from. I saw two state troopers coming down the hill Code 3, full lights and sirens. They pulled up right behind the deputy's car and got out. I could still hear more sirens. I glanced around to see where they were coming from, thinking it might be an ambulance. Nope, it was two Buffalo police officers. They were running Code 3 to aid another officer with a reckless driver. That was me. They helped me over to my therapist's office which was right next door to the hospital. I fell all over her office. I was screaming and yelling for her to come and help me.

The officers asked what I wanted to do, I said I needed to get to the hospital. When I walked into the hospital with eight officers, I remember the door opening, but that was it. I was in a coma for the next four days. I had no clue what was happening to me. I ended up in the St. Cloud hospital mental ward.

When I regained consciousness a man came into my room and told me he was there to help me with one of my problems. Well, I had lots of those. I had lost my family, my career, my business. My wife and I had lost our jobs and I had lost me. So I looked at that man and said, very smartly, "Which one would you like? I have all of these."

He said, "I want the drug problem."

I told him I didn't have a drug problem and they could only hold me for 72 hours.

He said, "Oh, I can take you to court and take your rights away." His name was Jed Right from Social Services of Wright County. He had tracked my drug use through my medical records. Jed Right saw that there were three overdoses and said he was going to take care of that problem one way or another. He offered me two things: 28 days in recovery or life in an institution. I couldn't bear being in an institution so I told him I would take the 28 days in recovery.

The next day Jed came back with paperwork for me to sign to put myself in recovery. I told him I didn't want to do it, that I had changed my mind and for him to get a judge, but then I thought about it really fast and told him never mind that I would go. I still had a massive amount of drugs in my system, I was far from being clean and the drugs were running through my veins. I was very scared because this was another place I would be locked into. I screamed at people trying to get them to let me call my wife.

Jed came back and took me into a room to sign the papers for the rehab program. I didn't know at the time how important it was, but I looked at Jed and said right to his face that I didn't care what they did to me, I didn't care if they beat me, raped me, hurt me or anything. I was going to make it no matter what they did. I was going to make it. I promised.

Jed looked at me with a smirk on his face and said, "I really hope you do." He was thinking that it was impossible for me to recover from what I had done to myself. He had seen this before with others in the past. But I was determined. I called my wife and asked her to bring my babies. I needed to see them. She brought them and I got to see them for about 15 minutes in my room.

I had gotten up and gone into the bathroom to wash my hair with hospital soap. It didn't work very well. It looked like I had poured grease on my head. I was 297 pounds and still swollen from the drugs. I looked horrible and scary. My girls didn't care though. They ran and hugged me and told me that they loved me. I told them I was going to get better, that the doctors were going to help me. I said, "Daddy is very sick, very sick."

They said, "Okay Daddy, we love you." I held them so tight and cried very hard. I tried not to let them see I was scared. I tried to hug my wife also but she didn't want anything to do with me. It was over. All she could do now was take care of our beautiful little girls. Surviving was what she had to do.

The girls went out into the hallway and my wife said to me, "I am not responsible for you anymore, and I'm sorry I ever got involved with a person like you. I'm sorry our daughters have to see this." And she left. As my family walked away I realized the door was locked. I stayed way back and waved to them as they left. I didn't want my girls to know that the door kept their dad in. I didn't want them to know I was locked up in there. I wanted them to think I was just getting help.

My wife came to the hospital the next day with clothes for me. I was suppose to go to Recovery Plus that day. I told the hospital staff that my wife would drive me over there. They said no, that I need to take a taxi. They were afraid that I would make my wife take me somewhere else and not to Recovery Plus. I would have tried it too, but by the grace of God I took that taxi and went to Recovery Plus.

Chapter Eleven

My wife met me at Recovery Plus with my suit case and went in with me. I was so scared. Thoughts went through my head, was I going to make it or was I going to die here?

I told my wife I loved her, I would miss her and I was sorry for everything. With tears in her eyes she said, "I am no longer responsible for you. I don't love you anymore, not this person you have become. I don't know you and don't want to."

I tried to hug her, but she said. "No." and walked away. I had destroyed this woman. A lady named Lucy came up to me and walked me down the hallway, the longest hallway of my life. I will never forget it. It seemed like ten miles but was only a few feet. Everything inside me was lost and out of control. I couldn't see or think straight. I couldn't talk. I couldn't control my emotions. I was crying every few minutes. I sat down in a chair and Lucy handed me some papers to fill out. Through my tears I told her I couldn't read or write very well. She said that was okay that she would read the questions and I could answer them.

REFLECTIONS OF A MIRACLE

When we finished I looked at Lucy and asked if I could please borrow her phone just for a second.

She said I couldn't because it was against the rules. I begged her, please. She finally relented and dialed my wife's cell phone. When my wife answered, I gently tried to tell her, "I'm gonna make it. I promise you I will make it. That is a guarantee. It will happen.

She said, "Sure, bye." and hung up. There had been so many lies and broken promises. How did I expect her to react? I handed the phone back to Lucy and just lost it. I was crying so hard. I looked up at that lady, crying and begging her to listen to me. I was going to make it, I didn't care what it took. "I'm going to make it. I promise you."

She said, "I hope you do."

I got to go out side and smoke my first cigarette in eight days. I had no money. My wife had given me a 250 minute phone card so I could call my girls. Twenty eight days, 250 minutes. That gave me eight or nine minutes a night to talk to my girls. I called my girls every night to say hi and to tell them I was doing okay. I was so scared that night I couldn't sleep. I lay there in bed watching the door, waiting for it to open.

I was in the V.A. Hospital to sleep and at Recovery Plus to get straight. Every thing left in me said to run, scream, hide. All I could think of was what was going to happen to me? What were they going to do?

Six AM came and there was a bang on my door. It scared me to death. There was a lady yelling, "Good morning." I got up, went to the sink and stuck my head under the faucet to wash my hair with soap. I had to step on the pedals to make the water work. I washed and combed my hair back. I grabbed the book the lady handed me and went out. I asked where I should go?

Several people were going down the hall and said, "Just follow us." They were people I didn't know, a bunch of low-life addicts who were scary and dangerous in my mind. I didn't want to be here around dangerous people. I followed very quietly. I went down stairs to a room where they said I could get something to eat for breakfast. A lady handed me a tag. I bought two yogurts and a coke with the tag. I sat by myself and ate as fast as I could.

People started to leave, so I followed them outside to a place where others were smoking. A van pulled up, I got in and we went over to Recovery Plus. When I got there, I asked people to help me find where I was suppose to go? I didn't know what

REFLECTIONS OF A MIRACLE

I was suppose to do. I was scared to death, hanging on by a thread, wondering what was going to happen to me, who was going to hurt me, were they going to lock me up?

They told me I had to see a man named Jake. They pointed to a door with a giant yellow smiley face on it. I knocked on the door. Thoughts were racing through my head, "It's over, my life is over. I have destroyed it. I have finally done what my dad did. I have become a miserable excuse for a person." I despise what he was and I refused to be like him.

A man opened the door, looked at me and said, "Can I help you?"

I said, "My name is Antonio," and I started to cry. I asked, "What do you want me to do? What do you want me to see? What do you want me to write? What do you want me to say? What do you want me to do? What? What? What?"

He looked at me with his eyes opened really wide and his hand out and said, "All I want you to do today for the whole day is breathe."

Breathe? Just breathe? I was doing that at the hospital. Why did I need to come here to do that? I could breathe. Hell, I'm addicted to breathing. Just breathe. So that's what I did. I went into his class and sat down. Everybody talked and when it came to my turn to say how I felt that day, I just cried. I did the same thing the next day and the next day and the next day.

Jed Right, my social worker, came walking down the hallway when I was walking around the corner and said, "Tony, I need to talk to you."

We went into the lunchroom and sat down. Jed said, "Listen, we have a problem."

I asked, "What's the problem?"

He said, "They don't want you here. They say you are too far gone, and they can't help you."

I looked at Jed scared to death and begged him to please give me some more time. I told him I was doing all that I could. He said he would give me three more days. That was on Friday. I had Friday, Saturday and Sunday. Monday morning I better have it together.

I said I would do it, no matter what I would make it. I promised. I was doing all I could. That night when I went back to the V.A. Hospital a big black man walked into the room and said we had an N.A. meeting to go to. I had no idea what that meant.

I later learned N.A. stood for Narcotics Anonymous. Someone told me we had to go into a room, sit in a chair and listen to someone talk. So I did. I sat in a big blue chair in the middle of the room in a half circle.

In walked this big giant biker – long black hair, biker black leather, goatee and sunglasses. I thought, "He's going to help me? He "invented" drugs. How would he help me? Help me get in trouble, help me learn something I didn't need to know, help me be mean, hurt someone, murder, what? What's he going to help me do?"

That big giant biker sat down and said, "My name is Patch and I'm a drug addict." Patch started telling his story. I thought, "Oh God, I'm going to hear this horrible, whining old man tell me how he went out hurting people in his biker days." But his story wasn't like that at all.

One thing in his story made a lot of sense to me. He said, "When I was drugging, if I had enough drugs, money and cigarettes, I knew I would be happy. So I got drugs, money and cigarettes, and I had lots of friends. All my friends had nicknames like FBI, DEA, Marshall, Sheriff and Police. All those friends showed up to help me. They helped me smoke my cigarettes, they helped me get rid of my drugs and my money, and then they took me away. I spent 42 months in prison. I saw the place where Timothy McVay was killed."

Patch swore that when he was in prison he would never do drugs again. He would get straight and stay straight. All he wanted was a job, a home, money, a phone he could answer and to be straight. So he started attending A.A. meetings in prison. When he got out, he started going to N.A. meetings. Patch said he had a phone he could answer; no one was searching for him. He had a bank account, and there was money in it. It was his, and he didn't have to worry. He had money, a home, a job and friends. No, they weren't just friends, they were something we were all looking for. They were family.

I thought to myself, "My God, if he could do it, I could do it." When he was finished I stood up out of my chair, walked over to him, put my hand out graciously saying thank you and wanting to shake his hand. He pushed my hand out of the way, hard, and wrapped his arms around me and hugged me.

The only thing that went through my mind was that he was a gay biker, too. I can't win. He whispered in my ear that I had "the look." He pushed me back away from him and looked at me, patted me on the shoulder and said, "Man, just hang in there. You got it. Hang in there."

He walked away and I ran back to my room, grabbed the picture of my family and held it against my heart. I lay down on my bed and begged God to help me.

In his story Patch kept mentioning his HP. I thought, "horse power" biker guy, you know. But as I was laying there, I finally realized as I was begging God to help me, that HP meant my Higher Power. I wondered right then and there that if there was someone up there looking out for me, then why did I suffer so badly? I stopped blaming God and I remembered what that biker guy had said.

I told that Higher Power, "No bull, if I sleep from 10:00 PM to 6:00AM and don't wake up with a bad dream, I swear to God I'll do whatever it takes to make it in this world. I want peace and happiness, and I will invite you into my heart forever. I woke up the next morning at 6:00 AM. I did not have one bad dream, and I had slept all night.

I was no longer the same person. I don't know what happened, and I don't care. All I do know and care about is that my Higher Power has looked out for me ever since then. He had kept me alive when I had tried to end my life. That hadn't worked, and there had to be a reason. I was looking forward to finding out what that reason was.

I wasn't really sure of anything much in my world at the time. Nothing made sense. I just kept getting up, moving forward. That was all I could do. The morning I woke up after a restful night was Saturday. We had A.A and N.A. meetings that lasted three or four hours. We had lunch and for the rest of the day we were free to do whatever we wanted.

I sat and thought about this Higher Power thing for a long time. I realized that it could all end soon, and I could be locked up for good come Monday.

I was awake and alive and had something warm inside my heart. Something very small, very tiny, telling me to move forward, to just keep trying, keep breathing, to just take it easy and not lose hope. I promised God, My Higher Power, that I would make it. God backed me up with a lot of power inside.

I'm not a very religious person, but I do believe in Heaven and God, and I believe in Hell and the Devil. My Higher Power has ridden with me, sat with me, talked to me and has stayed with me from that moment on. I was still scared so I mostly stayed in my room. My wife called on Saturday night. I asked her if she was bringing the girls to visit on Sunday? She hesitated. I begged her to please bring my babies. They were the one solid thing I had left to hold on to. I just wanted to see them in case I was locked up or committed on Monday. My wife agreed to bring the girls.

REFLECTIONS OF A MIRACLE

When my family arrived, I ran down the hallway because my babies were there to visit. I warned everybody as I ran past them to stay away from me and my family. I didn't want anything to do with anybody there. I wanted everyone to leave me and my family alone. When I got to the bottom of the stairs I looked up and there they were, my two little girls running at full speed, arms wide open screaming "Daddy."

I ran to them and hugged them tightly. I looked up to the sky feeling the warm sunshine on my face, and then I looked and saw my wife. What a beautiful woman. She was walking slowly across the yard. At that moment I begged God to give me back the one thing that was greatest in my life, my family. I tried to say nice things to my wife. I was trying to get her to understand that maybe something good could come out of all this. She told me that she was there only to let the girls see me, and that was it.

I sat there telling my girls, my beautiful little girls, that Dad was in recovery. I was trying to explain about my recovery, about the things I was doing. I even had a book and was trying to tell them that their daddy was coming back and that I would be even stronger and better than before. My wife sat a little ways from us. My wife and girls stayed 3 ½ hours. Finally my wife said it was hot out and she had 100 miles to drive to get back home. That was my wife. She drove 100 miles just so I could see my girls. I always said she was mean and asked how could she do and say the things she did to me. I realize now that it wasn't her. It was all the fog around me. I could never see through my own pain and suffering because I felt everyone was out to get me. I walked them out to the car. My wife got in the front, and I picked up my oldest daughter and squeezed her tight. I put my face in her hair and soaked in the smell. I told her I loved her and put her in the car. I wanted that smell to last seven days until I could see them again.

I turned around and there was my youngest looking up at me. She said, "Daddy."

I said, "Yes, honey?"

"Are the doctors here going to fix you?" Five years old and she wanted to know if Daddy would be fixed.

I told her the truth, "There is no cure for what Daddy has, but I feel something great, so you think about me, and I'll think about you. I love you very much."

I put her in the car and shut the door. I went to the front door. It was open so I leaned in to my wife and said, "I'm sorry." Tears poured out of her eyes under those sunglasses. It took everything I had to hold back my tears. I was a complete disaster and she knew it. This woman who was my backbone for so many years and who had tried to point me in the right direction, sat strong and tough there in front of me with tears running down her face. I didn't know what to say. There was no way for me to comfort her. I could not comfort my own wife. She had wanted to spend the rest of her life with me and all I had ever wanted was right there, but I had messed it up so badly I wanted to die.

She looked at me and said the words I will never forget, "How could you have done this to us? Why did you do this to us? I have to go." She put the car in reverse and as I got up out of the door frame, she shut the door and left. I ran into my room and lay down on my bed holding the picture of my girls. I screamed into the pillow and cried, begging God to help me so I could help them again. I begged him to help me be a better person, help me fight whatever it was that was trying to kill me, help me to move forward.

Monday morning rolled around, and I woke up a changed man. I can't describe it any other way. I wanted my recovery and there wasn't a dang thing going to stop me. I had told those people the first day I was there that I would make it, and I was going to do exactly that.

I walked into Recovery Plus and walked up to the first counselor I saw. I said, "I need to know every single thing there is to know about recovery. I want to know about meth, cocaine, marijuana, the prescription drugs, everything. Why did it make me sick? Why did I continue to take the pills? Why did I become an addict?"

I raised my hand every five seconds in class and asked all sorts of questions. I was going to do whatever it took. I fought everyday for my life. I wanted to be someone again – a person again. I wanted to get rid of the addiction that I had. I could never get rid of it, but I could hold it at bay, and I was willing to try.

I remember what my wife had said, "You can't help someone until they want to help themselves," and I wanted to help myself. Then everybody started helping me, everybody started seeing a new me. They said I was like a sponge. I soaked up all the information and wanted more. I was going to stay here. I asked God to please help me quit smoking, and I did quit for the entire time I was in recovery. The lack of money to buy cigarettes helped, too.

About the seventh day there, a lady walked in and stood there in front of us and said she had some bad news. I looked up at her thinking, "Bad news. Oh no. Someone has to go and it's going to be me." But, what the lady said was that a guy in recovery had left in the middle of the night. He had gone home and told his mom and dad that he wasn't doing well and was very upset. That night they all went to a birthday party, and he went downstairs in the basement, took a rope and hung himself. The guy could not handle his recovery.

That scared me even more, but it made me stronger. I was not going to give up like that. I was not going to leave my little girls without their daddy. I loved them too much.

I could make a life that was good and that I loved. I had one thing going for me- my Higher Power. I had God and He was willing to do whatever I needed to recover. Everyday I felt a struggle coming on, I also felt a warmth growing inside me. I began helping other addicts, and I wasn't even "fixed" myself yet.

There were days when I was so upset about that kid killing himself that I didn't know what to do. I asked counselors to help me. I was upset and crying for a man I had only known for two days. I didn't get a chance to shake his hand. I didn't get a chance hug him. I didn't get a chance to say, "Let me help you. You're going to be okay." I just didn't get a chance. Finally things started to make sense to me again. I was getting stronger. I was losing weight. I was losing weight so fast, it wasn't even funny.

One day I got a phone call. "Is this Antonio?"

"Yes, this is Antonio."

"This is Trooper Thomas from the Minnesota State Police."

I asked, "What can I do for you?" The accident I had had back when I had taken all the pills was now being investigated. I had left the scene of the accident to get to the hospital after my truck had been towed.

The officer asked what I was doing at the V.A. Hospital. I told him that I was in Recovery Plus in treatment for my drug addiction. I asked, "Are you going to write me a ticket for leaving the scene of an accident?"

Then came my second miracle. The officer replied, "Nope. I'm really glad that you're getting help and I wish you the best. You don't need anymore problems."

I said, "Thank you," and hung up. A few minutes went by and the phone rang again. I thought it might be my wife so I grabbed it. It was another Minnesota State Trooper. This was the partner of the one I had just spoken to.

He asked me the same questions, and I gave the same answers. I also asked him the same question.

He too, said I already had enough problems. He would not write me any tickets because I had made sure everyone was okay before I had left. I was so very happy.

I began seeing a therapist and told her about my childhood. She said, "I have to tell you something."

I said, "What's that?"

"You were not abused," she said.

I got so angry and said, "What do you mean I wasn't abused?"

She said in a small timid voice, "That wasn't abuse, it was torture. You were tortured and I'm very, very sorry all that happened to you."

I actually felt relieved. Someone understood how I had suffered and understood the pain I'd felt.

In no time I had made 28 days in recovery. I went up to Jake, the counselor, and said, " Hey, Jake. Do I bring my stuff tomorrow? I'm done. I made it 28 days." Everybody brought their stuff to class when they were done.

I had forgotten that I had made a deal with my social worker to do everything possible for my recovery. I had promised 28 days, and then I would go to a halfway house for 90 days to get it together so I could go back into the real world to be a productive citizen, to help others and myself.

Jake said, " You're not ready yet." I said, "Look, I signed on for 28 days. I'm good."

Jake said, "You're not ready yet."

I looked at him and said, "I am ready." We yelled back and forth, then I just shut up. I remembered something. They could lock me up at any time, and I didn't want to be locked up. Something inside me said to just shut up and let it go.

After a few minutes I turned to Jake and said, " I'm sorry, sir, for interrupting your class." I apologized in front of the whole class, but I did not cry. I said, "I'm sorry for pushing a man who knows my limitations." I didn't know them. I ended up spending 42 days in recovery and the V.A.

Finally the day came when Jake came to me and said, "Tony, listen. You're my miracle. I didn't think you would make it, but you did a very good job, and I'm very proud of you. Bring your stuff tomorrow." I was so happy that I went outside and cried. Then I got scared. I had to leave a place where I felt safe for the first time in my life. I was safe in a place that wasn't my home. But it was my home because God gave me my home right there and He made me happy. He gave me a chance to start my life again.

The next day I packed up my stuff to leave. I had borrowed a pick-up truck from my father so I could drive to the halfway house where I would stay for ninety days.

I walked out of Recovery Plus, got in the truck and drove to the stop sign at the end of the property. That uneasy feeling swelled up inside me. I looked over my shoulder at the Recovery Plus building. I remembered the first day I had said to myself that once I got out I'd never go back and now I was having a hard time leaving. Tears flooded my eyes. Those were my friends. No, they were my family. I was afraid I would never see them again, but then I remembered what Jake had said, "You can always come back."

Like before, it hurt but I had to move forward. So on to the halfway house I drove. It was early September. I was nervous but went anyway. I stayed all of September and did everything they asked me to do. I went through the steps, I did my paperwork, studied everyday, did all of my one-on-ones, and went to all my counseling sessions. I got a full time job and worked every Monday, Tuesday, Wednesday, Friday and Saturday. On Thursdays I attended my classes, my after school work, my adult education, saw my counselor and then went to my daughters' school to help in their classes for an hour. I got to see and hug my girls.

I didn't get mad, I just did what they told me to do and kept doing it right. I gave my wife $100 every Thursday. It was all the money I could give her. I studied really hard everyday. It was a new experience in a world I had never known.

Addicts are normal people. They just have a sickness inside of them that holds them back from doing things. Now I can do anything. I have God in my corner, and there is nothing greater. I had always had the greatest power in the world in me, but I just didn't know it. It was with me all of the time. Now I talk and pray "50 million times" a day thanking God for the gifts He has given me – my sanity, my health. I think everyday is the greatest day in the world.

In the halfway house I weighed 175 pounds. That was my second miracle. The weight was coming off. My counselors came to me several times questioning my massive weigh loss. They thought I was purging, going into the bathroom and throwing up after I ate, but I did not do that. I didn't need to. My Higher Power was helping me lose the weight. Some people thought the weight loss was the stress of losing my wife and children.

I attended the schooling, went to my after care and went to meetings. I was what they called a meeting maker. I went to the Mississippi Shake Down which is a big picnic for everyone. I went to the Candles

REFLECTIONS OF A MIRACLE

Under the Sea. I went to every single meeting, sometimes eight in a week. I went to A.A. and N.A. meetings. I had to do that if I was going to make it.

I wanted to build a family that had something in it that was better than anything I had known before. I wanted my family to have a Higher Power in it. My Higher Power is there for me everyday. I show my gratitude to my Higher Power by surviving in this world and being there for others who might need my help.

I started working for a construction company. I called my social worker and told him I needed him to give me my rights back because I had done really well and wanted to go over the road truck driving again. That was the way I thought I could get a home and money. I needed an apartment. I needed to leave this place and move forward in my life.

My Higher Power was backing me up all the way. Everything good was happening for me. My social worker laughed and said, " Tony, I told you if you did the 28 days and the three months in the halfway house, you could go. I never took your rights from you."

I said, "What?"

He anwsered," I didn't take your rights away. You were so messed up that you must have gotten confused and thought I really had. I never took them. You can leave right now if you want to, and by the way, you have done more than I ever expected. You have been a poster child to me, you helped me help other people. You are my success story."

I was thinking to my self, "Jeez, a miracle and a success story." Wow, all I really wanted was to live again. All I wanted was my life and family back. I wanted to fight for the good things in life. I called the halfway house and asked, "Can I graduate on October 21, 2004? I did. I was a free man again.

REFLECTIONS OF A MIRACLE

Chapter Twelve

I took an over the road truck driving job. Distance would help me or so I thought. I would call my wife and pick a fight with her just to hear her voice. She was so angry with me, and I just kept making it worse. I was working for this company for a couple of months but wasn't making any money. It was getting really bad. I couldn't help my wife and daughters with enough money to survive. I couldn't even talk to my wife she was so angry. I could talk to the girls every night, just not to her.

I got a sponsor when I was in the halfway house. When you have a sponsor, you are suppose to call them all the time. I could never reach him at home, so I got Nextel cell phones with the two-way walkie talkie feature, one for him, one for me. That way I could call him and get hold of him anytime. It worked out pretty well. I got teased a lot because none of the other guys in recovery ever bought their sponsors a phone. I guess I wanted it really bad. I know I did.

I would call my sponsor and tell him about how I was hurting and about how my wife was killing me from the inside. I tried everything I could, but it

REFLECTIONS OF A MIRACLE

didn't work for her. She wouldn't let things go. She just kept fighting with me.

My sponsor told me to take time and relax, to think of my Higher Power and let him guide me. It was hard, but I did it. As a professional driver, I drove thousands of miles. One night I hit an ice storm and called my wife. I begged her to listen to me. She asked, "What's the matter?" I said, "I'm scared. I'm in an ice storm, and I'm not sure what I'm doing. I want you to tell my daughters if anything happens to me that I am clean, I'm trying, I'm sorry and I love them very, very, much. Would you do that?"

She said, "Tony, honey listen. You are a great truck driver so relax and take it easy. You will make it, I promise." That was the first time she had said anything positive since I had walked into recovery.

I hung up the phone and looked to the side seat. I could almost see my Higher Power riding in the seat beside me.

I drove right through that storm with no problems and made the delivery on time. I called my wife back to say thank you, but she was again cool towards me. It was like a different person had answered the phone. I don't know what had happened.

Maybe it was my Higher Power working though my wife. She said yes, we had talked that night, but she had a different version of our conversation. It didn't matter though. I had made it through the storm.

I stopped working for that company and moved on to another. That company kept me in the lower southern states. I ran back and forth and was starting to make really good money. I was able to give my wife and daughters more money.

I kept asking my wife everyday if we could try to work things out? She said "No."

I called her every time I hit an anniversary of being clean. Thirty days – Can we work it out? Nope. Sixty days clean – Can we work it out? Nope. Ninety days clean – Can we work it out? Nope. Six months clean – "Hey baby, I got six months clean. What do you think?" She said, "Yeah, that's great." and hung up. I got nine months clean. "That's nice, great, you got nine months clean," but that was it.

I got eleven months clean and I called her. She answered, "What can I do for you?" She was always angry. I couldn't blame her. She was very hurt about what I had done to our life and about how she had to pick up the pieces and put it back together for our daughters all by herself. She was very cruel on the phone, but so was I. Sometimes I said things just to keep her on the phone.

REFLECTIONS OF A MIRACLE

She was helpful too because everyday she was mean to me, it made me ten times stronger. I was determined to be good for her and my girls. I would never give up. This time was different. I now had my Higher Power to help me.

One year clean I called my wife, "Hey, can you do me one favor?"

She asked, "What?"

I said, "Can you come when I get my one year medallion?"

She said, "I'll think about it."

At nine months, I had bought my first Harley Davidson motorcycle. I was also trying to buy a house near the one year mark. I was in town and went to the Mississippi Shake Down, an N.A. meeting. I rode my Harley to the meeting and parked it out front. I was just glowing. I had leather chaps, a jacket, gloves and glasses. I had made something of myself. I showed them all. In less than a year I had bought a Harley. I was proud. My son met me there.

This was the meeting I had asked my wife to come to. This was my one year medallion meeting. I sat there. They presented the 30 day medallions and the 60 day medallions, but she wasn't there. Then the 90 day medallions were presented. I turned and there they were, my wife and my sister-in-law. A year earlier my sister-in-law had told me on the phone that I was worthless and rotten for being messed up when I had taken care of her daughter. Her daughter never got hurt, but she was angry about what I had done to my family.

Yet here she was, one year later sitting in a chair looking at me one year clean. Actually she was staring at me in amazement. She couldn't believe that I had made it one whole year without alcohol or drugs. I had eleven people come up and say something to me that night. They told me how they remembered when I had walked in the doors what a mess I was. They talked about how I had walked up to people and asked how I could get my family back. I had begged help me, help me, help me get my family back. Everybody had told me to relax and breathe to sit down, take a number, and go to more meetings. I had done just that. They told me what a great person I had become. They talked about how much I had helped others and how they looked forward to seeing me at the meetings. They said I had inspired them with their own fights and struggles for survival, and I felt really good.

Then my wife stood up and walked to the middle of the circle with me. I said, "My name is Tony, and I'm a recovering addict. Everyone in the room said, "Hi, Tony."

Then my wife said, "I'm Kay, and I'm Tony's wife."

After everyone said, " Hi, Kay," you could have heard a pin drop. Kay looked at me and with tears in her eyes said the words I will never forget: "I am proud of you. I'm proud that you don't feel the need to sink yourself away into drugs. I'm proud of our son for being here to stand by your side." She hugged me and my son and walked back to her seat.

She was proud of me, proud of me – an addict, a loser, someone that I thought didn't matter anymore in her world, and she was proud. That lit a fire inside of me that couldn't be put out. I didn't want to. I wanted to keep going. That was July 12, 2005. One year clean.

On September 28, 2005 I was driving through town and wanted to see the girls. I called and asked my wife to meet me at McDonald's. She said okay. I drove my semi to McDonald's and parked. I talked to the girls a little while outside at a picnic table. I asked my wife if she would come to the truck to talk with me. She agreed. We sat in the truck and talked. Again it was the, "Why did you do this to us?" I didn't have an answer.

I leaned in to kiss her like I use to do and she didn't pull away. She kissed me back. I held her in my arms and asked if we could please try again? I promised that this time I wouldn't let her down. I swore it.

Of course, with my track record, those were empty words, but she said, yes. I finally had a chance to have my family back. Now I was even more determined to do everything I could to mend the damage I had done. So much damage. I couldn't change the past, but I could prove my self to her in the future. I was so proud to be with her again, I could barely contain myself. I hadn't been with anyone else since she and I had split up.

Kay is a great person who had a lot of pain inside, but she was willing to come back and try after all I had done to her, after all that I had destroyed in her world, after all I had taken from her. She had been blissfully in love with me for the first seven years, but I had turned into a mindless monster. But now, Kay was willing to give me a another chance.

REFLECTIONS OF A MIRACLE

Chapter Thirteen

I started going to Recovery Plus when I was six months clean. I still share my story and hope I can help someone else like that other speaker did for me. I hope that I can light a fire in someone else so they can conquer own their addiction.

I go one Friday a month and spend two to three hours speaking. I don't tell every detail of my story, but I give them enough to let them know that I came from a bad place but pulled myself up with a little help along the way.

My wife has come to hear me speak three or four times. She tries to blend in with the crowd. It's a different group every time. But once I hold up the pictures and we take a smoke break, they start to look around. One or two may notice that she looks familiar.

At the end of my story, I tell everyone that I am so lucky to have someone like her. I say, "I will probably get in trouble for this, but she is right here," and I point to her. She usually turns red as she stands up. They give her a standing ovation. A lot of them come up and hug her and tell her what a wonderful person she is, and they tell me what a inspiration I am to them. I couldn't ask for more.

I met my wife when I was 30 years old and she was 20. That's when my life began. A lot of water has gone under the bridge and there are still a lot of problems, but we keep working on them. The road home is a long one, but worth every mile. I truly believe this woman is my soul mate. I want to be with no other person in this world.

My family is my third miracle.

My fourth miracle is my partner in business. A man I barely knew put such trust in me. I went to him with a business plan and on my word he invested $250,000 in my plan. We are now partners in a successful business. He believes in me. I am so lucky that someone believes in me again.

My Higher Power is always looking out for me. It's one day at a time now. I take life one day at a time and just breathe. I am living proof that there are second chances in life. Living proof that you can sink so far down but still be saved. I am so clear now. I see better, hear better, and feel better than I ever have in my life. I thank God everyday and I cherish every moment with my family.

I now weigh 163 pounds. I am no longer bloated and swollen from the excessive drugs in my system.

Some say I have lost a whole other person. I have no flabby skin from the weight loss, no stretch marks, nothing. I am a fortunate man.

I am proud to say that for thirteen years I have had two people who are all my parents should have been. I respect them and look to them for guidance. These people are my in-laws. The most wonderful parents in the world. They welcomed me back into their family with open arms. They encourage me and praise my accomplishments. I hope one day I can be just like them.

I want to thank everyone who has helped me along the way. Those people are my miracles. If this book helps one other person in this world with his or her own struggle, it's all worth it. If there's anyone out there, no matter what you are suffering from or if you're scared and need help, don't take the easy way out. Ask for the help you need. Tell someone close to you, someone you can trust. Real friends won't desert you. Tell a cop, ask a fireman, go to a hospital, and tell the truth. Tell the truth, it will set you free. I am living proof there are second chances in life. All you have to do is ask for it.

REFLECTIONS OF A MIRACLE

YO-EIH-720

Getting Started

You will need the following information to register with Train & Assess IT for the first time:

✔ A **30-character Train & Assess IT access code**, which is included in your Train & Assess IT Student package. Open your Train & Assess IT package and pull back the cardboard strip on the inside to reveal your student access code.

✔ An **8-character Course Section ID** provided by your instructor. If you don't have it yet, contact your instructor.

✔ A valid **e-mail address**. If you don't have one, contact your school's technology center or set up a free account on a Web site that offers this service (for example, Hotmail or Yahoo!).

Train & Assess IT User's Guide

PEARSON
Prentice Hall

Upper Saddle River, New Jersey 07458

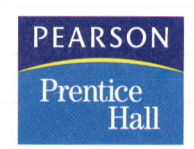

Student Technical Support

Web: 247.prenhall.com

E-mail: online.support@pearsoned.com

Phone: 1-800-677-6337

Copyright © 2006 by Pearson Education, Inc., Upper Saddle River, New Jersey, 07458.
Pearson Prentice Hall. All rights reserved. Printed in the United States of America. This publication is protected by Copyright and permission should be obtained from the publisher prior to any prohibited reproduction, storage in a retrieval system, or transmission in any form or by any means, electronic, mechanical, photocopying, recording, or likewise. For information regarding permission(s), write to: Rights and Permissions Department.

This work is protected by United States copyright laws and is provided solely for the use of instructors in teaching their courses and assessing student learning. Dissemination or sale of any part of this work (including on the World Wide Web) will destroy the integrity of the work and is not permitted. The work and materials from it should never be made available to students except by instructors using the accompanying text in their classes. All recipients of this work are expected to abide by these restrictions and to honor the intended pedagogical purposes and the needs of other instructors who rely on these materials.

Pearson Prentice Hall[TM] is a trademark of Pearson Education, Inc.

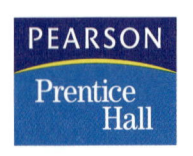

10 9 8 7 6 5 4 3 2
ISBN 0-13-236859-5

User's Guide

Contents

About the User Guide iv
System Requirements iv
Installing Train & Assess IT iv
   Install the Partial Local Install 1
Installing the Macromedia Authorware Web Player 7
   Check Browser Type and Version 7
   Install the Authorware Web Player for Internet Explorer . . . 7
   Install the Authorware Web Player for Netscape 9
Signing in to Train & Assess IT for the First Time 14
   Complete Student Self-Registration 14
   Register with Pre-Assigned Student Account 18
Using Train & Assess IT 21
Training Walkthrough Overview 22
Assessment Walkthrough Overview 24
Using the Train IT CD 26
Getting Help and Support 27
   Student Guide 27
   Contact Professor 27
   Contact Tech Support 28

About the User's Guide

Train & Assess IT is a software application that allows you to hone your skills and demonstrate your proficiency in Microsoft Office 2003 applications, including Word, Excel, Access, and PowerPoint, as well as Computer Concepts, Internet, and more. This user guide is intended to get you up and running on Train & Assess IT quickly, so that you can focus your time on learning new skills.

Student Technical Support
Web: 247.prenhall.com
E-mail: online.support@pearsoned.com
Phone: 1-800-677-6337

System Requirements

- Web browser (Internet Explorer 5.01 or higher *or* Netscape 4.7 or higher)
- Macromedia Authorware Web Player
- Live Internet connection (56K minimum connection speed required)
- Pentium Class or higher CPU, 133 MHz or faster
- 16 MB RAM (32 MB recommended)
- 32-bit operating system (Windows XP, Windows 2000, Windows NT 4.0 with Service Pack 3, Windows ME)
- Screen resolution of 800x600 or greater, 256 colors or greater (some training lessons require screen resolution of 1024x768)

Installing Train & Assess IT

The Partial Local Install (PLI) CD(s) included in this package contain the Train & Assess IT software that should be installed on any computer on which you plan to take tests using Train & Assess IT. In addition to installing the PLI, you will also need to install the Authorware Web Player for your browser.

In a campus computer lab: If you use Train & Assess IT in your campus computer lab, the Train & Assess IT Partial Local Install and Authorware Web Player may already be installed on the lab computers, ready for your use.

To determine if the Train & Assess IT Partial Local Install is already installed, look for the Train & Assess IT icon on the computer lab desktop or the PH Train & Assess IT item on the All Programs menu. If you do not find either of these items on your computer, check with your instructor or campus computer lab administrator to determine if you should install the Partial Local Install and the Authorware Web Player on the lab computer. If instructed to do so, please follow the steps below to complete the installation.

At home or other location: If you access Train & Assess IT from home, work, or another computer not located in a campus lab, you will need to install the Partial Local Install and the Authorware Web Player to run Train & Assess IT. Please complete the following steps to complete the installation.

Installation Tips:
- Be sure to close all other applications before beginning the installation, including your antivirus program.
- If you are planning to install testing and training, be sure you have time to complete the installation before you start. The installation could take approximately 5 to 20 minutes, depending on which products you are installing and the speed of your computer.

Install the Partial Local Install

1. Insert the Partial Local Install CD (labeled PLI or PLI 1 in your package) into your CD-ROM drive.
2. When the InstallShield Wizard starts, click the **Next** button.

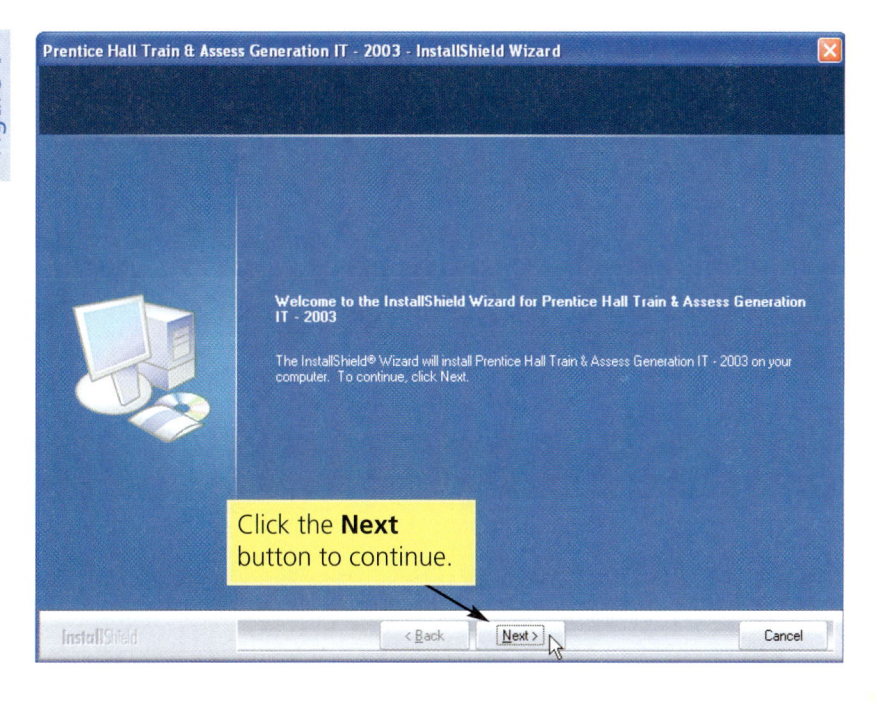

Figure 1

[Screenshot of Prentice Hall Train & Assess Generation IT - 2003 - InstallShield Wizard showing welcome screen with annotation: "Click the **Next** button to continue."]

If the Train & Assess IT CD does not start automatically, complete the following steps:

1. Click the Start button.
2. Click Run on the Start menu.
3. Type **D:\setup.exe** (where D is your CD-ROM drive).
4. Click the OK button.

3. Read the license agreement. To accept the terms of the license agreement and continue the installation, click the **Yes** button. (If you click the **No** button, setup will close.)

Figure 2

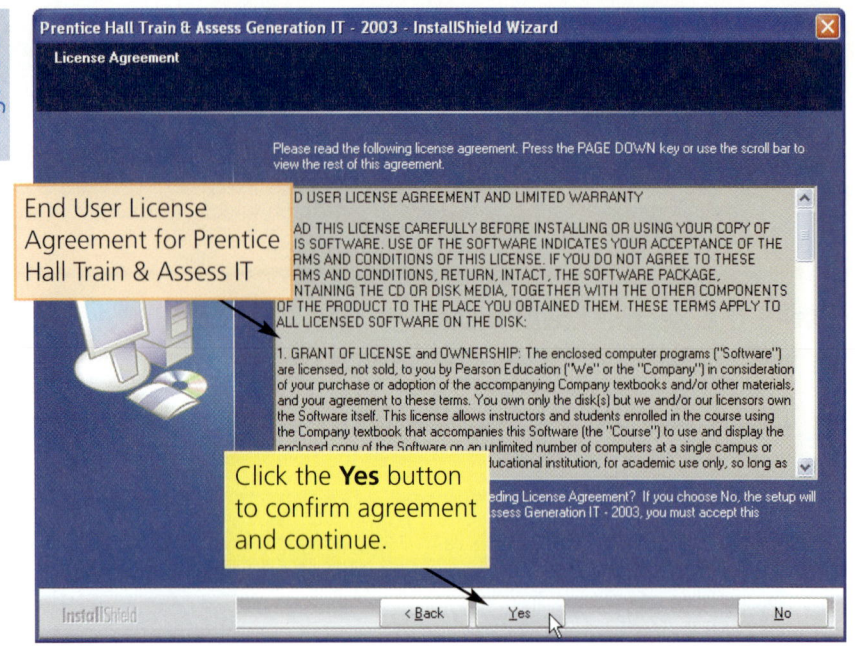

[Screenshot: License Agreement dialog of Prentice Hall Train & Assess Generation IT - 2003 - InstallShield Wizard]

- End User License Agreement for Prentice Hall Train & Assess IT
- Click the **Yes** button to confirm agreement and continue.

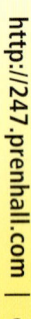

4. Next, you will be prompted to choose a destination location where setup will install the Train & Assess IT files. Unless your instructor instructs you to install Train & Assess IT to a different folder, accept the default location by clicking the **Next** button.

Figure 3

[Screenshot: Choose Destination Location dialog showing default folder C:\Program Files\PH Train & Assess IT\]

- Default destination folder location selected
- Click the **Next** button to accept the default location and continue.

http://247.prenhall.com | 2

5. Next, you will be prompted to choose what content to install on your computer. By default, **Testing** is selected, as it must be installed on your computer to run Train & Assess IT.

   Optionally, you can choose to install **Training** on your computer. If you have a slow Internet connection, installing Training on your computer will improve the performance of Train & Assess IT. If you have limited space on your computer hard drive, install Testing only.

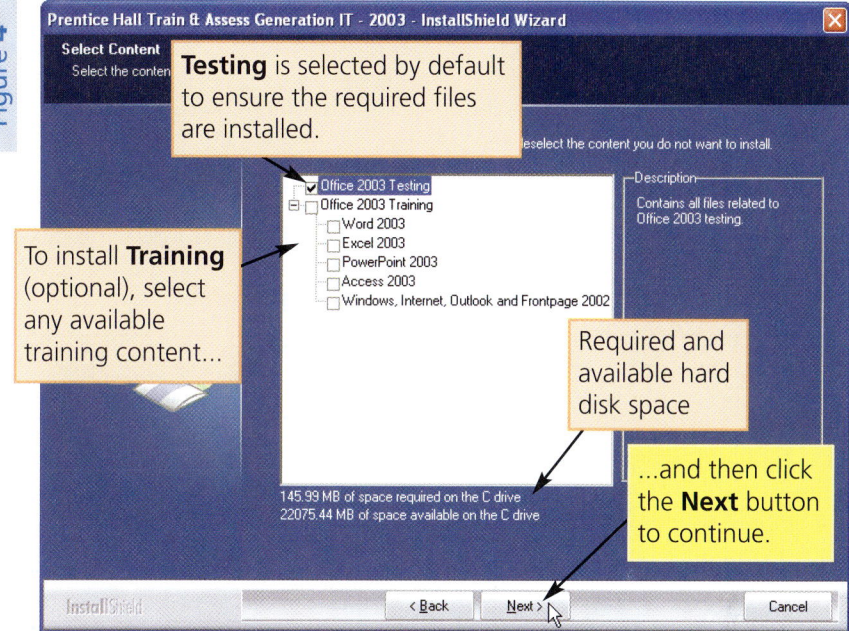

Figure 4

Testing is selected by default to ensure the required files are installed.

To install **Training** (optional), select any available training content...

Required and available hard disk space

...and then click the **Next** button to continue.

Unsure how much hard drive space is available on your computer?
As shown in Figure 4, Train & Assess IT setup indicates how much hard disk space is required to install the selected files for Testing and/or Training, as well as how much hard disk space is available.

Note to Train & Assess IT Essentials Users: If you are installing the Train & Assess IT Essentials PLI, PLI 1 contains the Train & Assess IT testing software, which is a required installation, and the Train & Asess IT Level 1 training files, which you have the option to install. PLI 2 contains the Train & Assess IT Level 2 and Level 3 training files, which are an optional installation.

If you wish to install the optional training files on your computer, continue through the steps to finish installing PLI 1 (Steps 1 through 9) and then again complete those steps to install PLI 2. **Please check with your instructor before installing the training files on your computer.**

user's guide | 3

6. When the Web site screen is displayed, confirm that the Address is **http://www.phgenit.com** and then click the **Next** button.

Figure 5

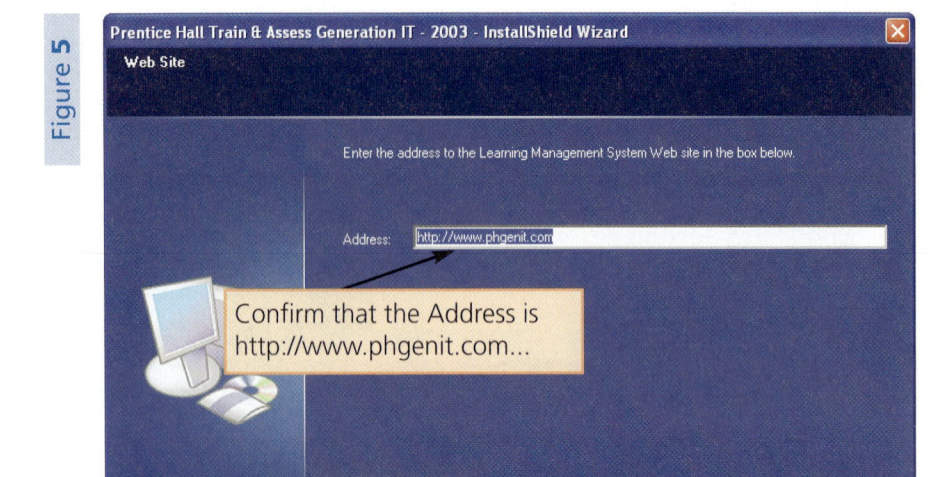

Confirm that the Address is http://www.phgenit.com...

...and then click the **Next** button to continue

7. When prompted whether or not to create a shortcut to Train & Assess IT on your desktop, click the **Yes** button.

Figure 6

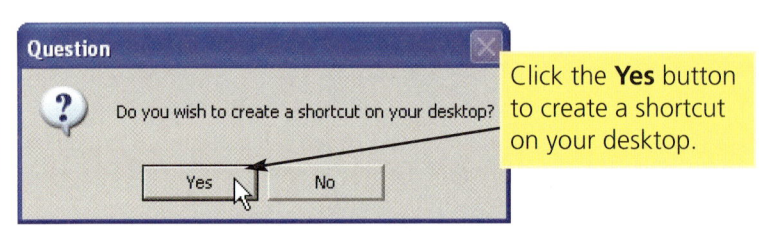

Click the **Yes** button to create a shortcut on your desktop.

Needed for additional help installing your PLI? For detailed installation instructions specific to your Partial Local Install, visit our Student Technical Support Web site at **http://247.prenhall.com** and then search using the keywords "Train Assess" to view all Help articles related to Train & Assess IT. Look for the article specific to your PLI (for example, GO! with Microsoft Office 2003 PLI Installation Instructions).

8. Setup is now ready to copy files needed to install Train & Assess IT. Click the **Next** button to begin copying files.

Figure 7

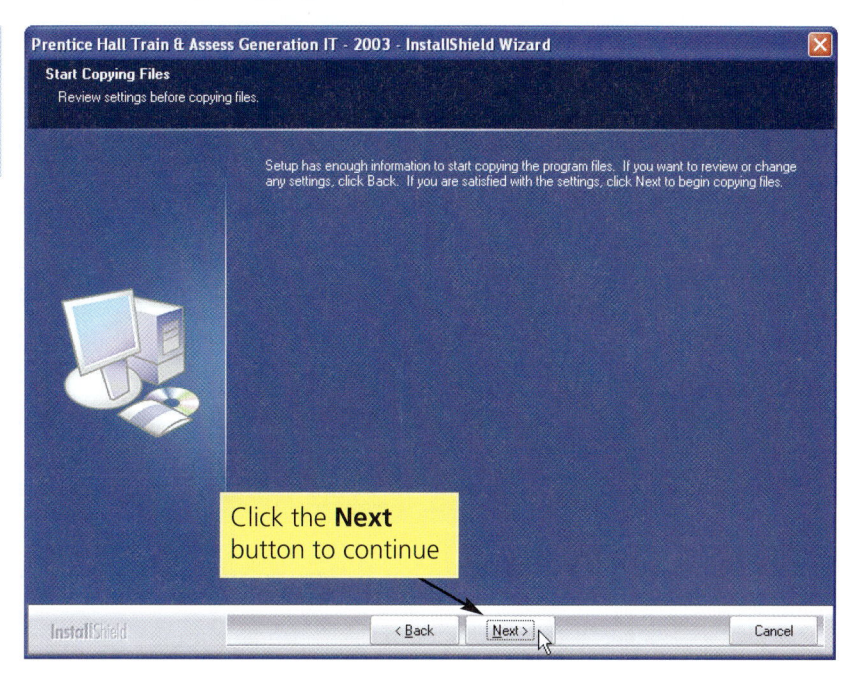

*Screenshot of "Prentice Hall Train & Assess Generation IT - 2003 - InstallShield Wizard" Start Copying Files dialog. Callout: "Click the **Next** button to continue" pointing to the Next button.*

9. The InstallShield Wizard will display a window showing the status of the installation (Figure 8a). When the InstallShield Wizard complete screen appears, the installation has completed successfully (Figure 8b). Click the **Finish** button to complete the installation.

Figure 8a

Screenshot of Setup Status window showing installation progress. Callout: "The status bar indicates progress of installation" pointing to the progress bar.

user's guide | 5

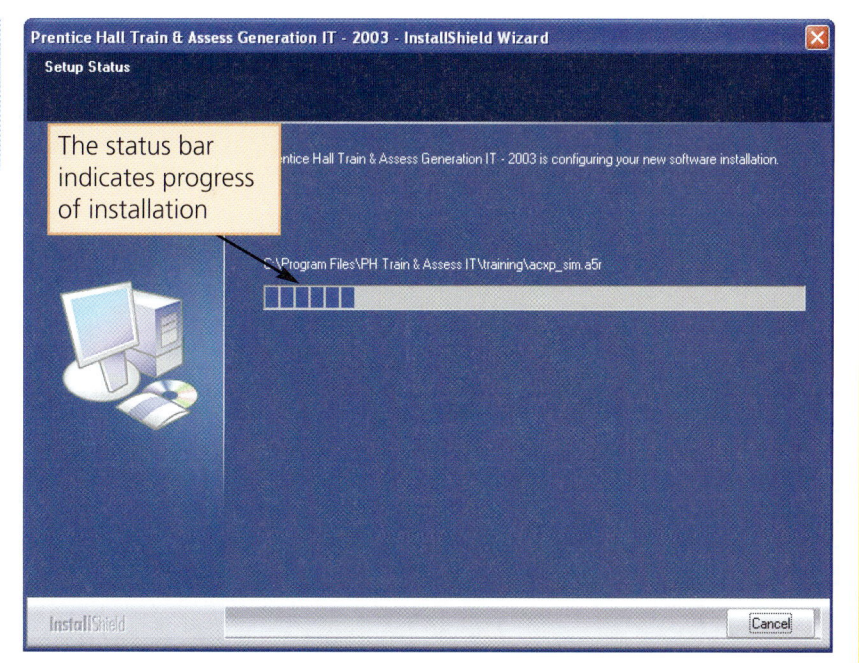

Figure 8b

[Screenshot: Prentice Hall Train & Assess Generation IT - 2003 - InstallShield Wizard, InstallShield Wizard Complete screen]

Click the **Finish** button to complete installation.

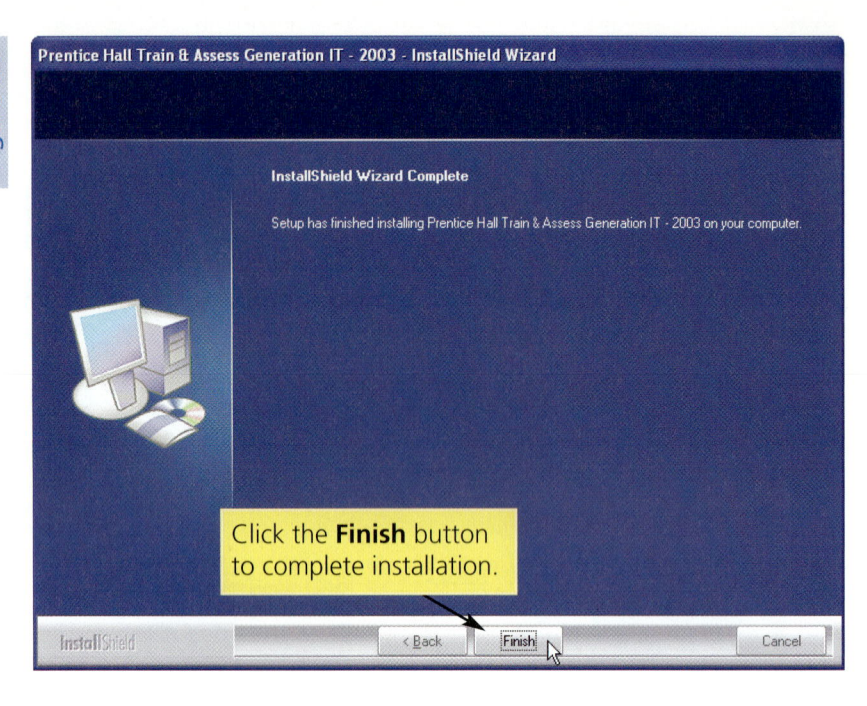

10. With your computer connected to the Internet, double-click the Train & Assess IT icon on your desktop to launch the Train and Assess IT PLI. The Train & Assess IT home page will appear in the PLI window, as shown in Figure 9. To close the PLI, click the **Close** button on the PLI title bar.

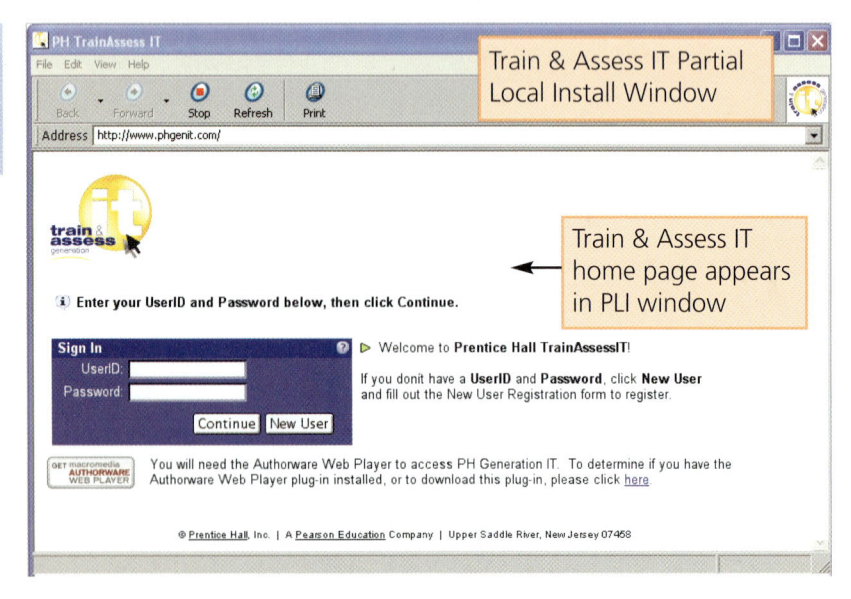

Figure 9

[Screenshot: PH TrainAssess IT window showing the Train & Assess IT home page with Sign In form]

Train & Assess IT Partial Local Install Window

Train & Assess IT home page appears in PLI window

http://247.prenhall.com | 6

Installing the Macromedia Authorware Web Player

Next, you must install the Authorware Web Player, which is a plug-in used to play the testing and training content in Train & Assess IT.

Check Browser Type and Version

Before you get started, make note of which Web browser version you are using. To determine what Web browser version you are using, complete the following steps:

1. Start your browser.
2. When the browser window opens, click **Help** on the menu bar and then click **About Internet Explorer** or **About Netscape**.
3. The browser will display version information for your browser (for example, Internet Explorer 6.0 or Netscape 7.2). Write this information down and then follow the steps below for your browser — either Internet Explorer or Netscape.

Using America Online (AOL)? We recommend using either Internet Explorer or Netscape outside of the AOL® service when using Train & Assess IT. If you are using AOL 4.0 or above, Internet Explorer is already installed on your computer. [You can download the latest version of Internet Explorer at AOL Keyword *Browser* or you can download the latest version of Netscape at AOL Keyword *Netscape*.]

After you have Internet Explorer or Netscape installed, sign on to AOL. Minimize AOL by clicking the minus sign (-) in the upper right corner and then start Internet Explorer or Netscape. You are using AOL as your connection to the Internet, but you will be using another browser to view and navigate Train & Assess IT. Follow the steps below to install the Authorware Web Player for your browser.

Install the Authorware Web Player for Internet Explorer

1. With your computer connected to the Internet, type **www.phgenit.com** in the browser Address bar and then press the ENTER key.

2. When the Train & Assess IT home page is displayed, click the **Get Macromedia Authorware Player** button.

   The AutoInstall Macromedia Authorware Web Player window appears (Figure 10). The program installer automatically will begin the Authorware Web Player installation.

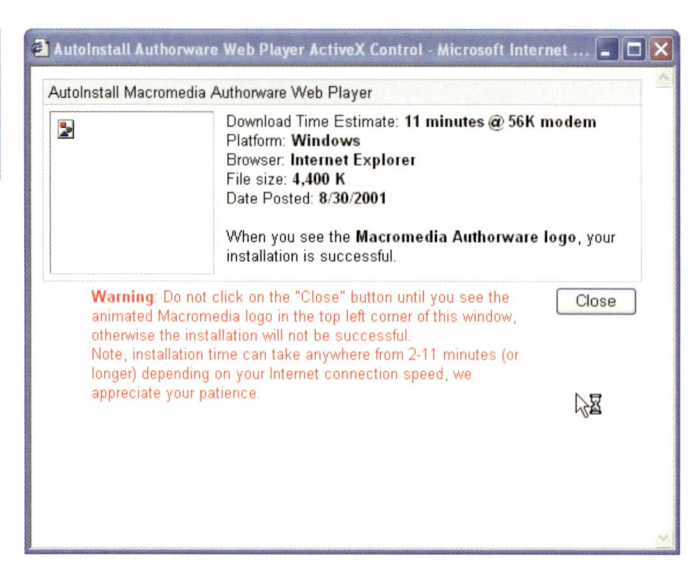

   Figure 10

3. After a few minutes (wait time varies depending on the speed of your Internet connection. 56K modem connections take approximately 11 minutes to complete the install), a Security Warning dialog box appears, asking for permission to run the Authorware Web Player control. Click the **Yes** button to continue.

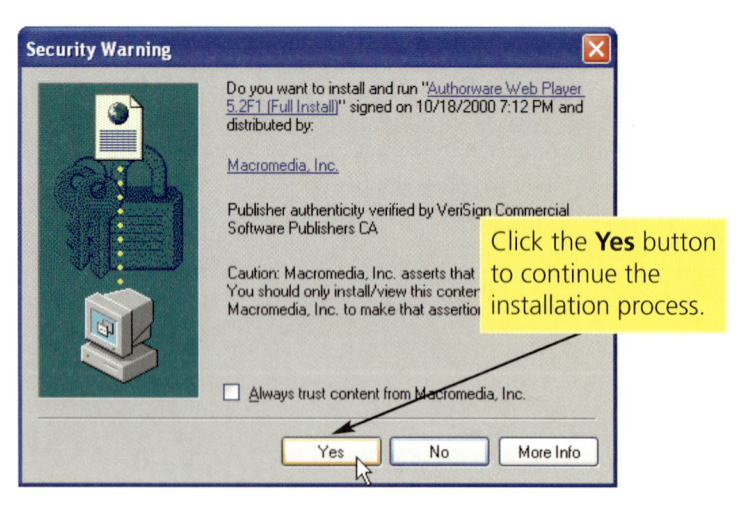

   Figure 11

   Click the **Yes** button to continue the installation process.

4. After a few minutes, the AutoInstall window will display a graphic with a green wavy line (Figure 12), indicating the installation of the Authorware Web Player is complete. After you have verified that the installation is complete, click the **Close** button to close the AutoInstall window.

Figure 12

When the Macromedia logo shows "is installed" and a green wavy line, Authorware Web Player installation is complete.

After installation is complete, click the **Close** button to close the window.

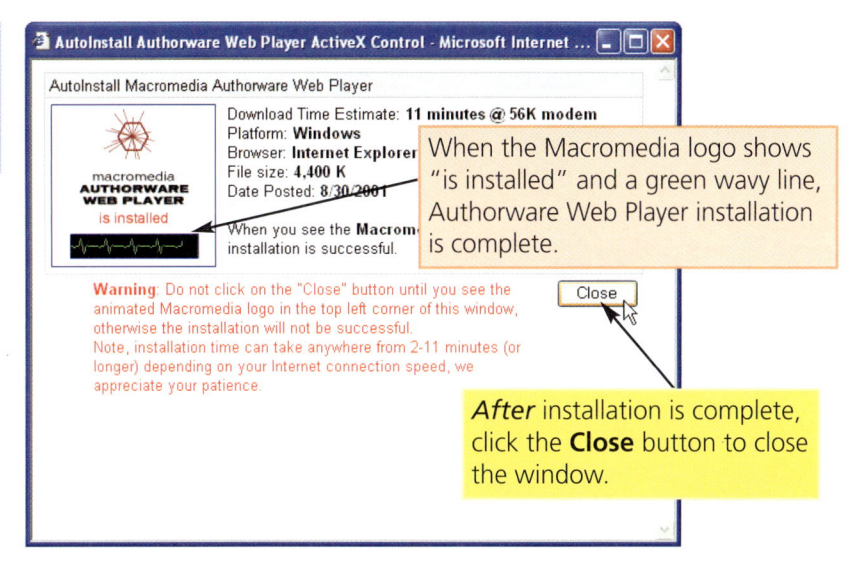

Install the Authorware Web Player for Netscape

1. With your computer connected to the Internet, type **www.phgenit.com** in the browser Address bar and then press the ENTER key.
2. When the Train & Assess IT home page is displayed, click the **Get Macromedia Authorware Player** button.
3. When the Download Authorware Web Player – Netscape window opens, click the **Get Macromedia Authorware Player** button.

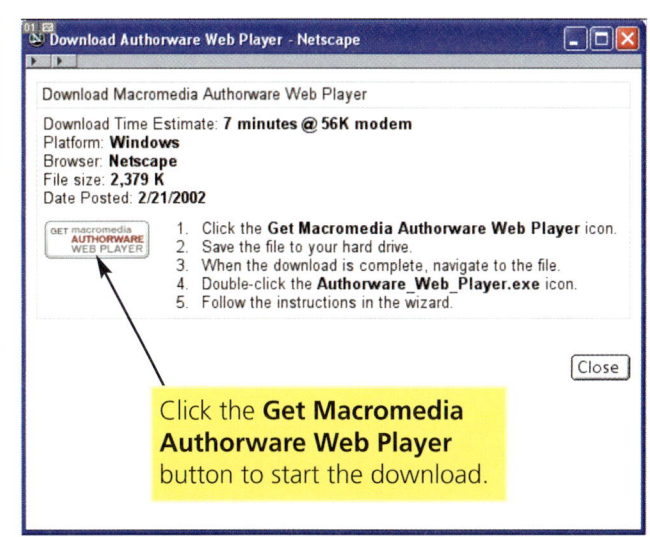

Figure 13

Click the **Get Macromedia Authorware Web Player** button to start the download.

user's guide

9

4. When the Opening Authorware_Web_Player.exe dialog box appears, click the **Save it to disk** option button and then click the **OK** button.

Figure 14

If necessary, click the **Save it to disk** option button...

...and then click the **OK** button to start the download.

5. A dialog box appearss and prompts you to save the Authorware_Web_Player.exe installer to a specific directory or folder on your computer.

    To download the installer to your Windows desktop, click the **Desktop** icon and then click the **Save** button. [If you choose to download the installer to a different location, make a note of the directory to which you are saving the installer, as you will need to find it to begin the installation.]

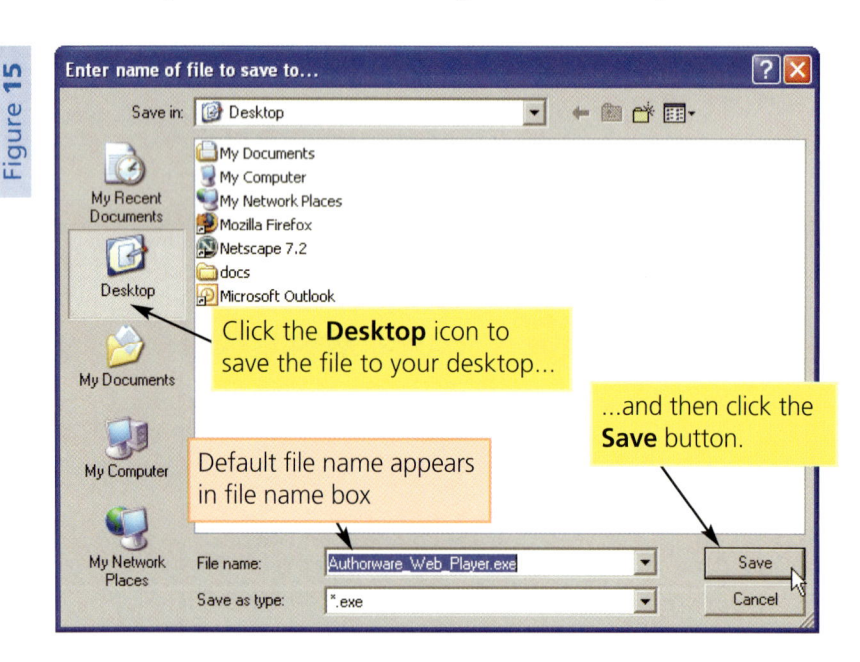

Figure 15

Click the **Desktop** icon to save the file to your desktop...

...and then click the **Save** button.

Default file name appears in file name box

http://247.prenhall.com | 10

6. After the Authorware_Web_Player.exe file has finished downloading, if necessary, click the **Close** button to close the Download Manager window.

Figure 16

Progress of **Finished** indicates the file download is complete.

Click the **Close** button to close the Download Manager window.

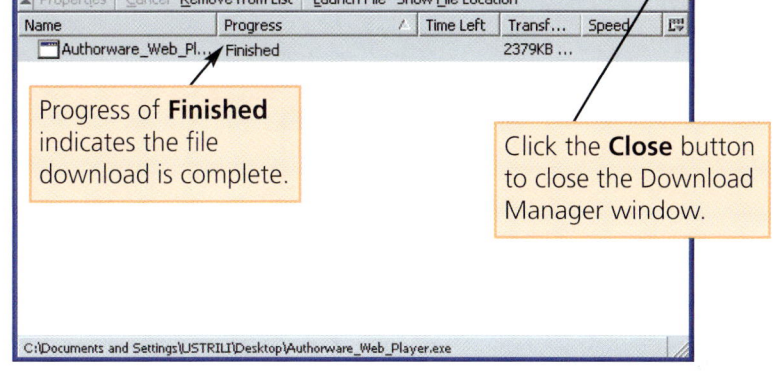

7. Next, locate the Authorware_Web_Player.exe file on your Windows desktop [or other location where you saved the file] and double-click it to begin the installation.
8. When the Authorware Web Player Installation screen appears, click the **Next** button to continue.

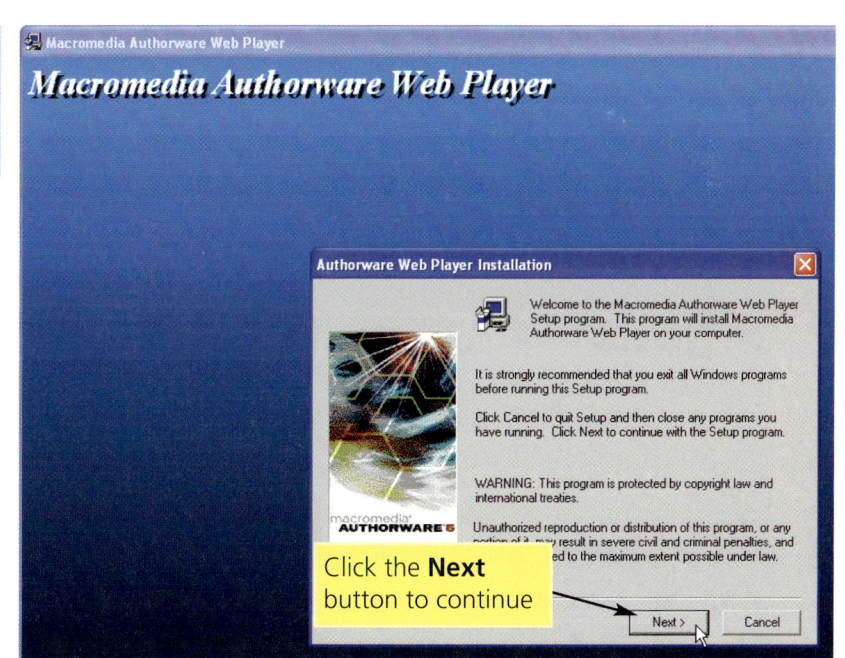

Figure 17

Click the **Next** button to continue

| user's guide

11

9. Read the license agreement. To accept the terms of the license agreement and continue the installation, click the **Yes** button. (If you click the **No** button, setup will close.)

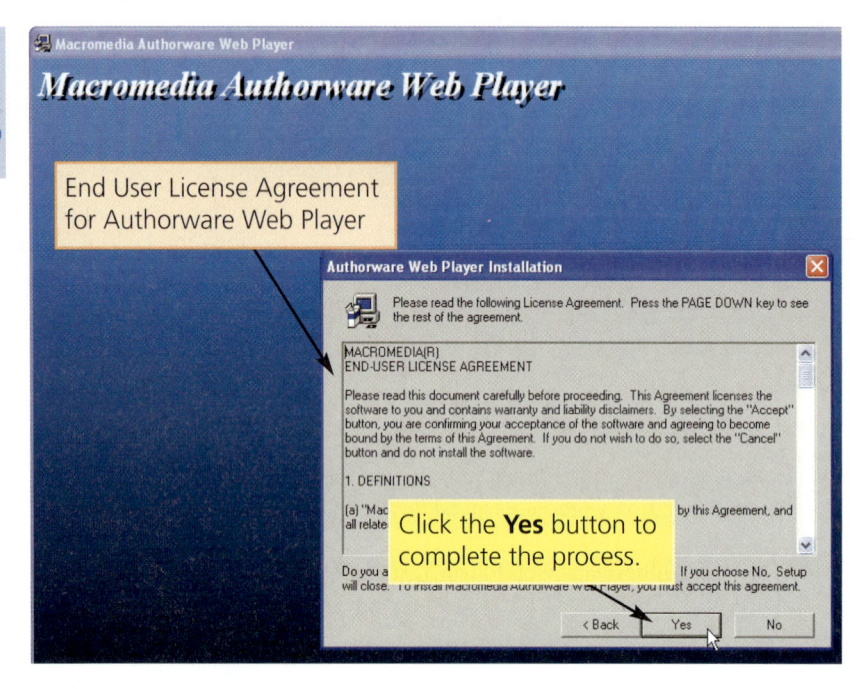

Figure 18

End User License Agreement for Authorware Web Player

Click the **Yes** button to complete the process.

10. When prompted, select your browser type and version from the list of available browsers (Figure 19). Be sure to select the correct version of Netscape. Click the **Next** button.

Figure 19

Select the correct version of your Web browser from the list...

...and then click the **Next** button to continue

11. Click the **Next** button to accept the default installation directory (unless your instructor instructs you to use a different directory).

Figure 20

Accept the default installation directory...

...and then click the **Next** button to continue

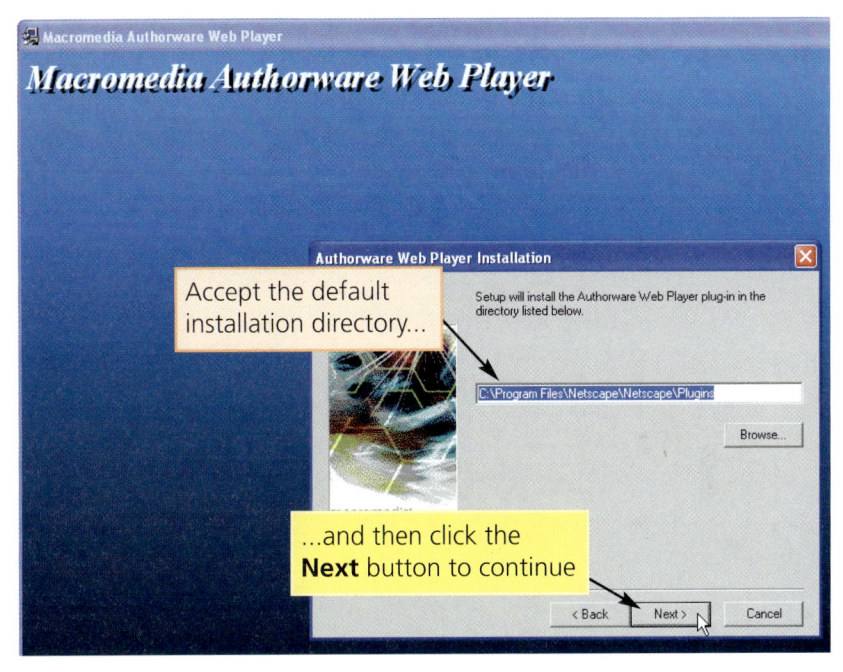

12. A status bar will appear, indicating the progress of the installation (Figure 21).

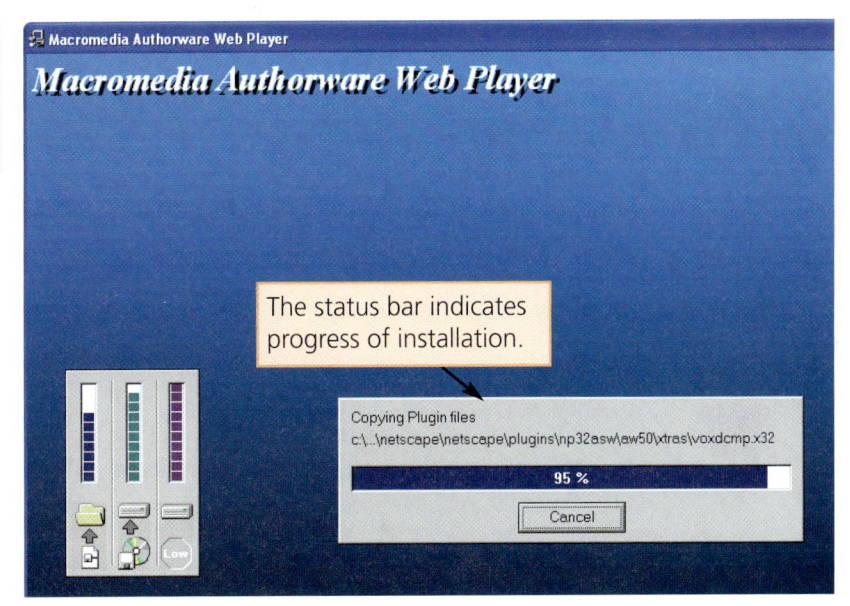

Figure 21

The status bar indicates progress of installation.

| user's guide

13. When the Setup Complete window appears, click the **Finish** button (Figure 22). *The installation of the Authorware Web Player is complete.*

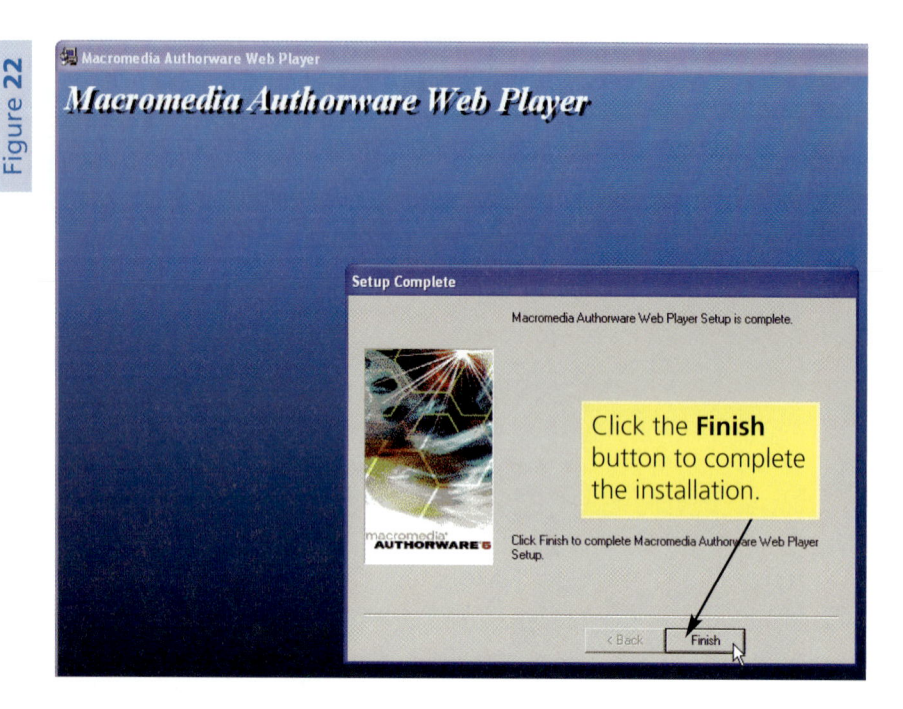

Figure 22

*Click the **Finish** button to complete the installation.*

14. Click the **Close** button on the Download Authorware Web Player - Netscape window to close this window.

Signing in to Train & Assess IT for the First Time

Depending on how your instructor has set up your course section, you may be asked to (1) self-register and create your account or (2) register with a pre-assigned student account. If you are not sure which steps to follow, contact your instructor for more information.

Complete Student Self-Registration

1. To complete the self-registration process, you will need the following three items:
   (1) A **30-character Train & Assess IT access code**, which is included in your Train & Assess IT Student package. Open your Train & Assess IT package and pull back the cardboard strip on the inside to reveal your student access code.
   (2) An **8-character Course Section ID** provided by your instructor. If you don't have one, contact your instructor.
   (3) A valid **e-mail address**.

2. With your computer connected to the Internet, launch the Train and Assess IT PLI (Partial Local Install). To launch the PLI, you can either:
   - Click the Train & Assess IT icon on your desktop; or
   - Click the **Start** button and then click All Programs on the Start menu. Click PH Train & Assess IT on the All Programs menu and then click Train & Assess IT.

> *Note:* If you do not have the PLI installed, start your Web browser, if needed. With your computer connected to the Internet, type `www.phgenit.com` in the browser Address bar and then press the ENTER key.

3. When the Train & Assess IT Sign In page appears (Figure 23), click the **New User** button to begin creating your student account.

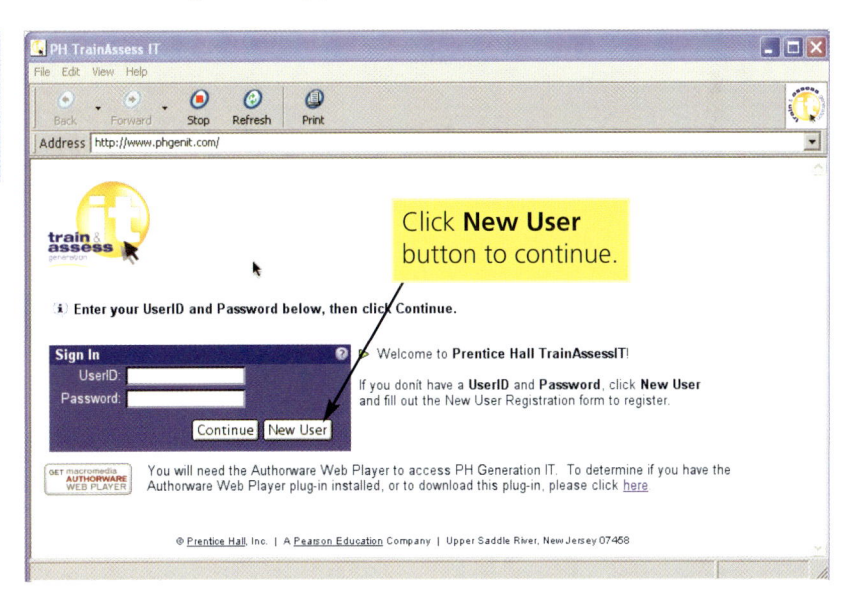

Figure 23

Click **New User** button to continue.

4. Next, complete all fields on the New User Registration screen (Figure 24 on the next page). You will need to enter:
   - Your first and last name;
   - A unique User ID and password that you will use to sign in to Train & Assess IT in the future;
   - The 8-character Course Section ID provided by your instructor;
   - Your 30-character Train & Assess IT access code;

   After entering this information, click the check box to confirm that you agree with the License Agreement. (Note that all fields, including e-mail address, are required.)

Figure 24

Enter your registration information...

Click the **Next** button to continue.

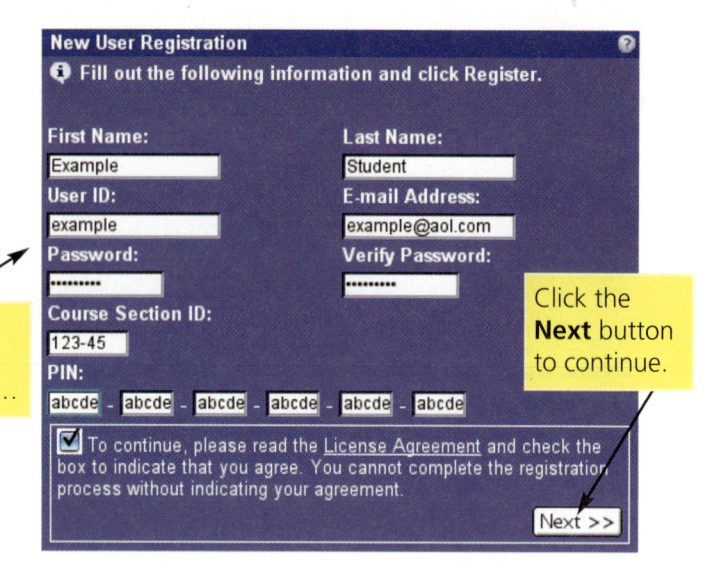

5. After entering all data, click the **Next** button to continue. If an Internet Explorer dialog box appears, as shown in Figure 25, click the **Yes** button.

Figure 25

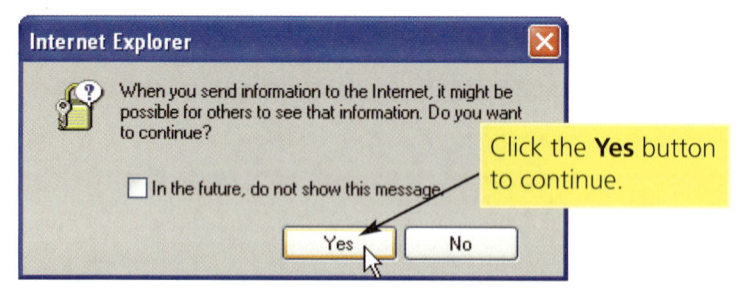

Click the **Yes** button to continue.

6. A confirmation screen is displayed to verify your registration information. If desired, print this screen for your records (be sure to keep it in a secure place so others do not have access to your user name). Click the **Register** button to continue.

Figure 26

Click the **Print** button to print a copy for your records.

Click the **Register** button to continue.

http://247.prenhall.com | 16

7. If one or more Internet Explorer dialog boxes appear, click the **Yes** or **OK** button to continue. When the Security Warning dialog box appears (Figure 27), click the **Yes** button to complete the registration process.

Figure 27

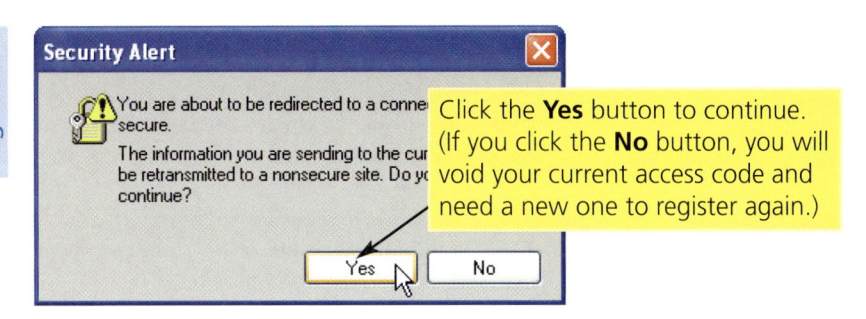

Click the **Yes** button to continue. (If you click the **No** button, you will void your current access code and need a new one to register again.)

Note: You *must* click the **Yes** button in the Security Warning dialog box to successfully complete the registration process. If you click the **No** button, you will void your current access code and need a new one to register again. In the event this happens, please contact Technical Support at online.support@pearsoned.com or 1-800-677-6337.

8. Congratulations! You are successfully registered and logged into Train & Assess IT (Figure 28). The next time you log in, enter the User ID and password in the Sign In box and then click the **Continue** button.

Figure 28

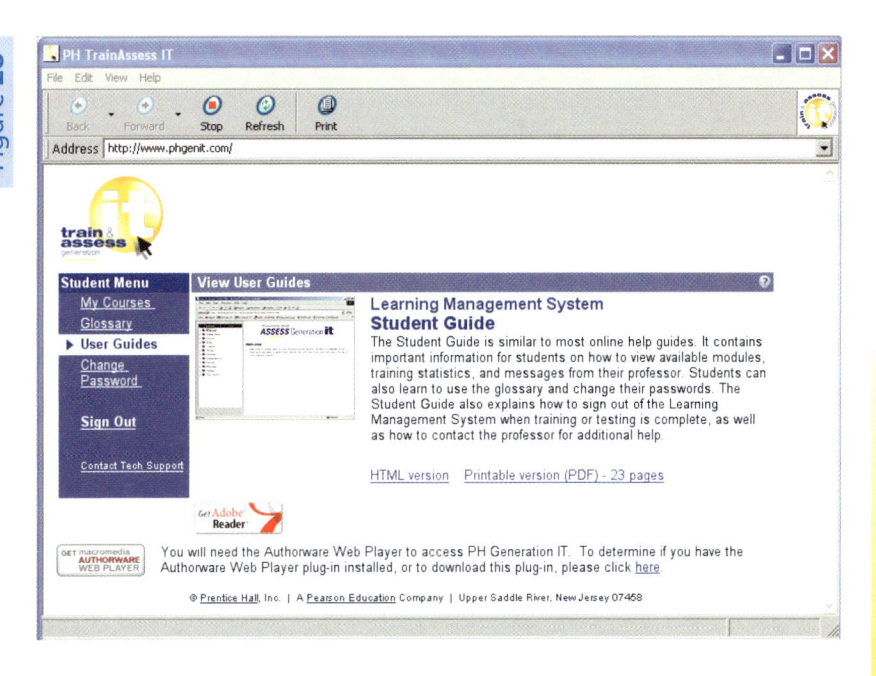

| user's guide

17

Register with Pre-Assigned Student Account

If your instructor has already set up your student account, s/he will have provided you with a User ID and password to complete the process of activating your pre-assigned student account.

1. To complete the account activation process, you will need the following two items:
   (1) A **30-character Train & Assess IT access code**, which is included in your Train & Assess IT Student package. Open your Train & Assess IT package and pull back the cardboard strip on the inside to reveal your student access code.
   (2) The **user ID** and **password** provided by your instructor.
2. With your computer connected to the Internet, launch the Train and Assess IT PLI (Partial Local Install). To launch the PLI, you can either:
   - Click the Train & Assess IT icon on your desktop; or
   - Click the **Start** button and then click All Programs on the Start menu. Click PH Train & Assess IT on the All Programs menu and then click Train & Assess IT.

> *Note:* If you do not have the PLI installed, start your Web browser, if needed. With your computer connected to the Internet, type **www.phgenit.com** in the browser Address bar and then press the ENTER key.

3. When the Train & Assess IT Sign In page appears (Figure 29), enter the User ID and password assigned to you by your instructor and then click the **New User** button.

Figure 29

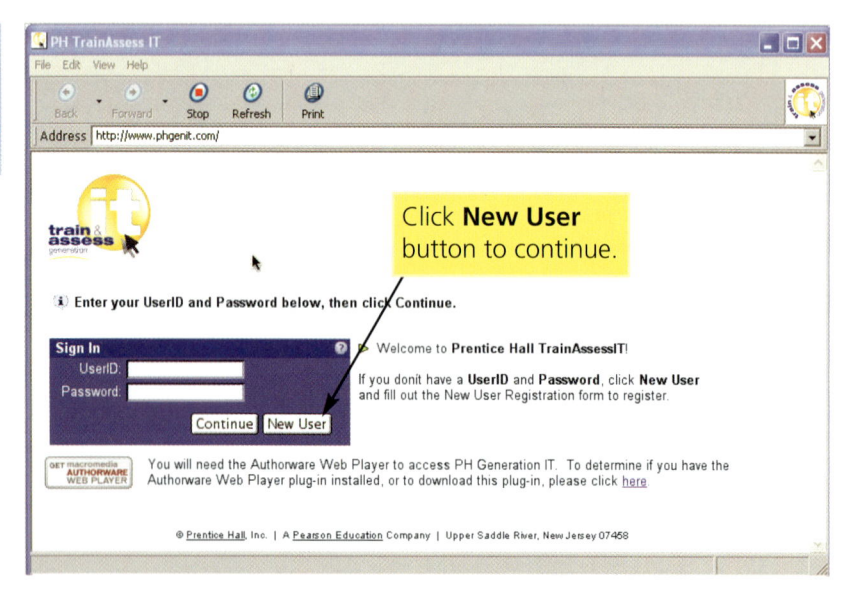

Click **New User** button to continue.

4. When the New User Registration screen appears, enter your 30-character Train & Assess IT access code and then click the check box to confirm that you agree with the License Agreement.

Figure 30

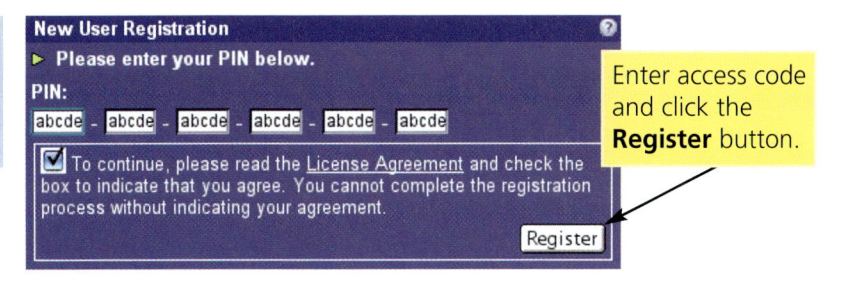

Enter access code and click the **Register** button.

5. Click the **Register** button to continue. If an Internet Explorer dialog box appears, as shown in Figure 31, click the **Yes** button.

Figure 31

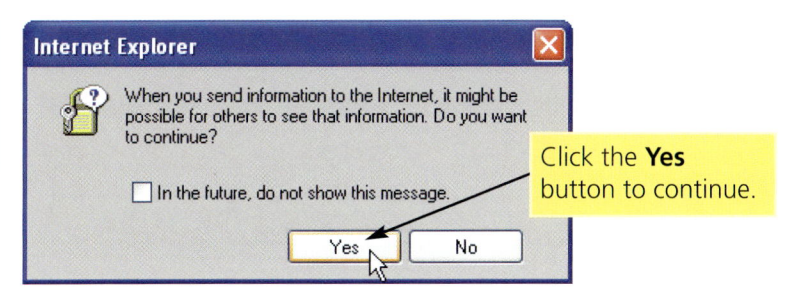

Click the **Yes** button to continue.

6. If one or more Internet Explorer dialog boxes appear, click the **Yes** or **OK** button to continue. When the Security Warning dialog box appears (Figure 32), click the **Yes** button to complete the registration process.

Figure 32

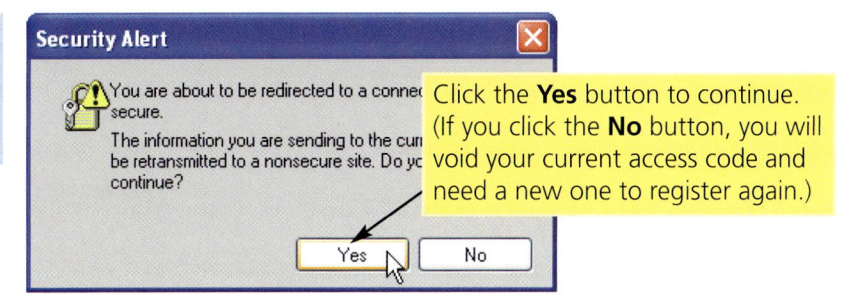

Click the **Yes** button to continue. (If you click the **No** button, you will void your current access code and need a new one to register again.)

| user's guide

> *Note:* You **must** click the **Yes** button in the Security Warning dialog box to successfully complete the registration process. If you click the **No** button, you will void your current access code and need a new one to register again. In the event this happens, please contact Technical Support at online.support@pearsoned.com or 1-800-677-6337.

7. Congratulations! You are successfully registered and logged into Train & Assess IT (Figure 33). The next time you log in, enter the User ID and password in the Sign In box and then click the **Continue** button.

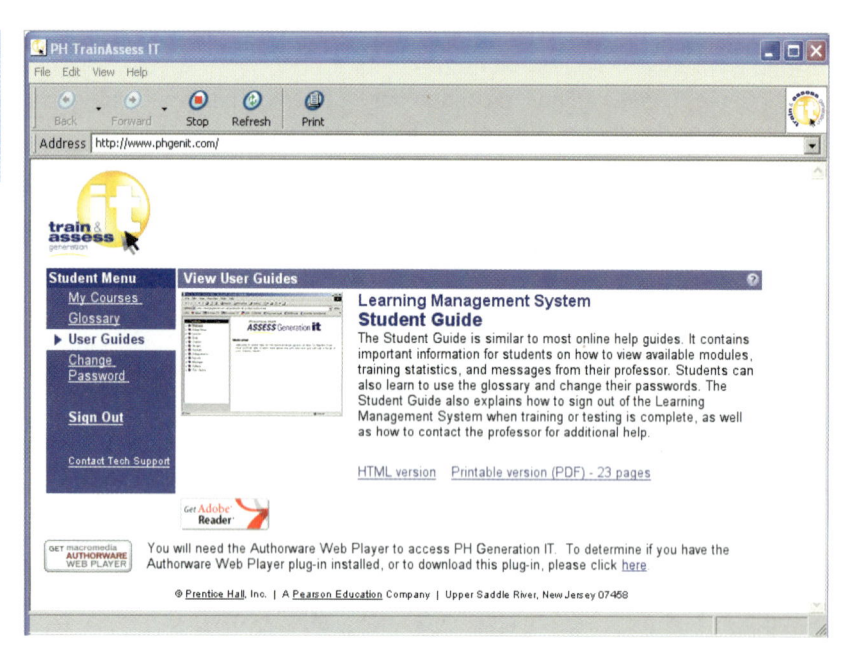

Figure 33

Using Train & Assess IT

Train & Assess IT is designed to be easy to use and navigate, so that you can complete your learning tasks efficiently. All of the main areas of Train & Assess IT are listed in the navigation menu at the left side of the page. This section describes the main areas in Train & Assess IT to help you get started quickly.

My Courses	When you first log into Train & Assess IT, the **My Courses** page appears, listing any courses in which you are currently enrolled. To view assignments for a course, click the course name.
My Modules	When you click a course name on the My Courses page, the **My Modules** page for that course appears. The My Modules page lists any training or testing modules assigned by your instructor.
My Statistics	The **My Statistics** page allows you to view and send your results on the assigned tests and training modules for your course.
My Messages	The **My Messages** page allows you to view and send messages from the instructor of the course you have entered. The My Messages page lists messages by subject and date sent. You also can sort messages on the page.
Glossary	Confused by a term used in either the training or testing? The **Glossary** allows you to locate and view vocabulary terms and definitions. The Glossary contains terms for all the modules in PH Train & Assess IT, organized in alphabetical order. To find a definition for a term, search for the term or click the first letter of the word to browse the glossary.
User Guides	The **User Guides** page includes links to the Train & Assess IT Student Guide, which includes information on how to view available modules, training statistics, and messages from an instructor. The User Guide also explains how to change your password and use the glossary.
Change Password	The **Change Password** page allows you to change your Train & Assess IT password at any time. To change your password, you will need to enter your current password, enter your new password twice, and then click the Submit button.
Sign Out	When you are finished working in Train & Assess IT, you should sign out so that others cannot complete activities using your account. Clicking the **Sign Out** link in the navigation menu will end your Train & Assess IT session. You can sign in again at any time to start a new Train & Assess IT session.

Training Walkthrough Overview

The following section describes and shows how to start, navigate, and exit a Training lesson. Note that your training interface may appear slightly different depending on the version of Office you are using.

To access an assigned training lesson, click on My Modules, click on your Course Section name, and then click the name of the assigned Training lesson. The training lesson will launch in a new window.

Many training lessons start with one or more slides that cover key concepts, followed by slides where you will be asked to practice hands-on skills and review concepts. Figure 34 and Figure 35 (on the next page) show important navigation tools and areas of the training interface.

Figure 34

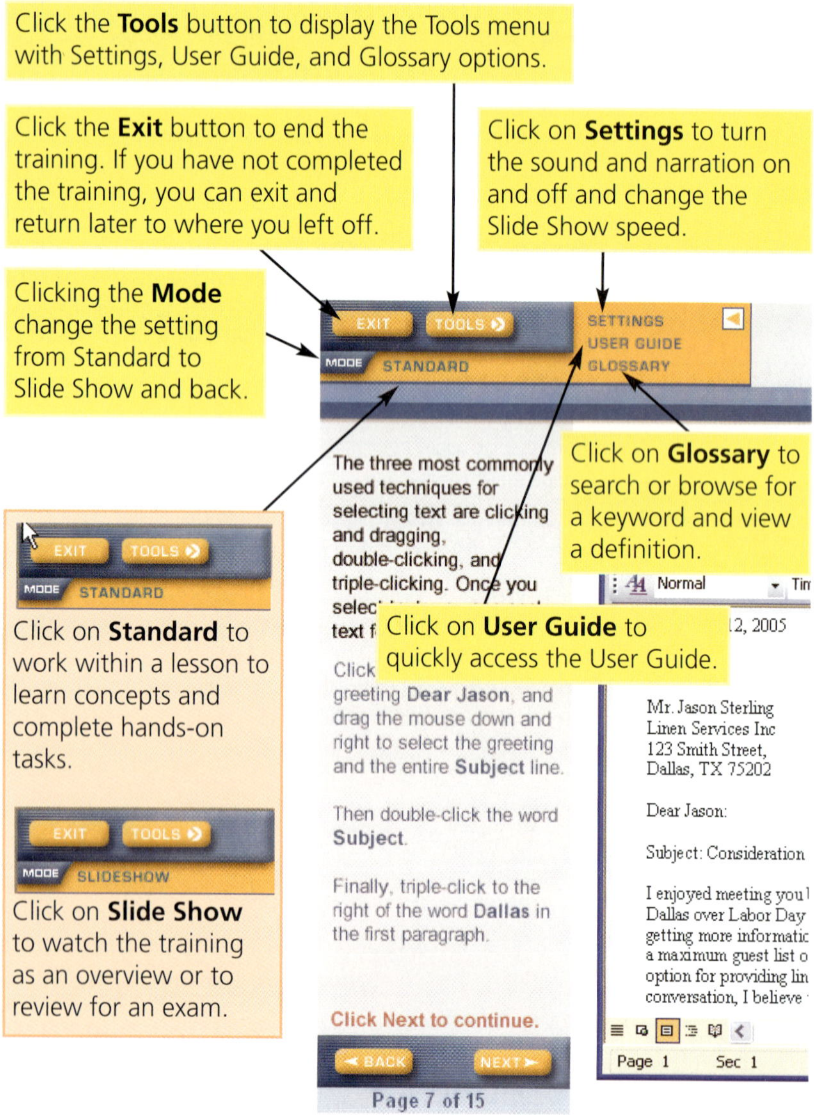

Click the **Tools** button to display the Tools menu with Settings, User Guide, and Glossary options.

Click the **Exit** button to end the training. If you have not completed the training, you can exit and return later to where you left off.

Click on **Settings** to turn the sound and narration on and off and change the Slide Show speed.

Clicking the **Mode** change the setting from Standard to Slide Show and back.

Click on **Standard** to work within a lesson to learn concepts and complete hands-on tasks.

Click on **Slide Show** to watch the training as an overview or to review for an exam.

Click on **Glossary** to search or browse for a keyword and view a definition.

Click on **User Guide** to quickly access the User Guide.

As shown in Figure 34, you can complete a training lesson in one of two modes: Standard or Slide Show. To select the mode of training you would like to work in, click the **Mode** button to change the setting. Each click will change the mode to one of the following:

- **Standard:** Work within a lesson to learn concepts and complete hands-on tasks.
- **Slide Show:** Watch the training for a quick overview or to review for an exam.

If you want to end a training lesson before you have completed it, click the **Exit** button. If you have not completed the entire module, you can exit and then later return to the training lesson.

Figure 35

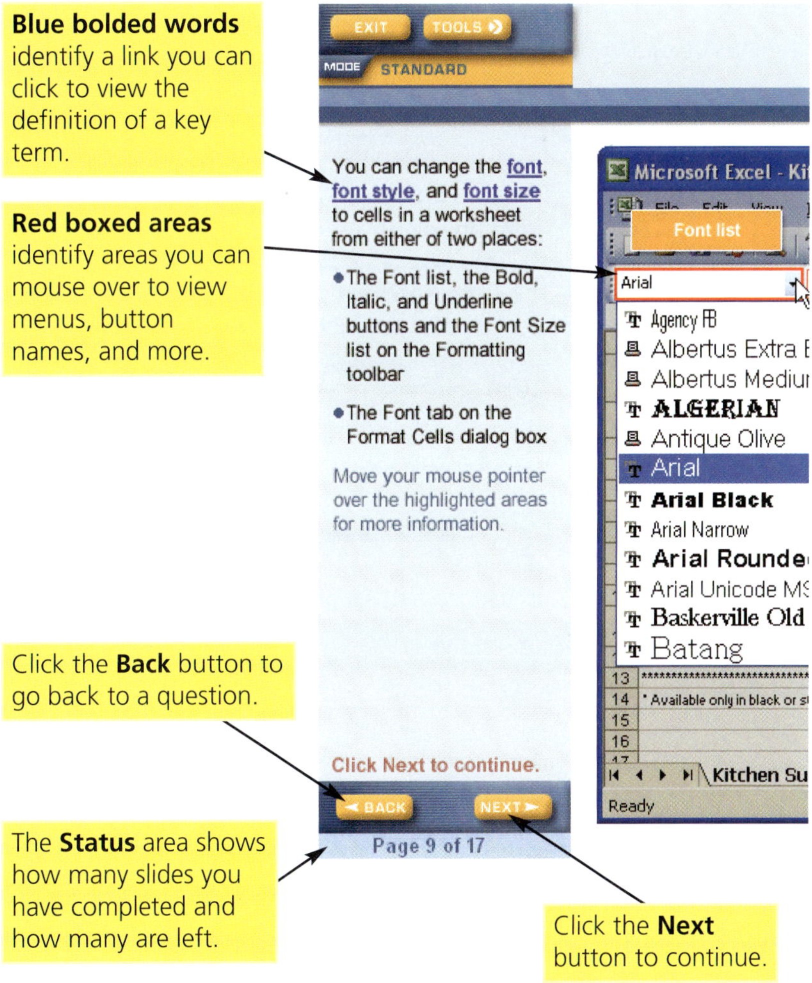

Blue bolded words identify a link you can click to view the definition of a key term.

Red boxed areas identify areas you can mouse over to view menus, button names, and more.

Click the **Back** button to go back to a question.

The **Status** area shows how many slides you have completed and how many are left.

Click the **Next** button to continue.

Assessment Walkthrough Overview

When taking a test in Train & Assess IT, you will be able to answer the questions by actually performing the tasks within a simulation of the actual application. Before taking an assessment or test in Train & Assess IT, you should familiarize yourself with the testing interface. Figure 36 shows important navigation tools and areas of the testing interface.

Figure 36

Click the **Question List** button to display a list of all questions in the exam. You can select another question from the Question List and then move directly to that question.

The **Status area** lists the topic being covered, percent of questions complete, which question you are viewing, and the time spent in the test (if your instructor has enabled these features).

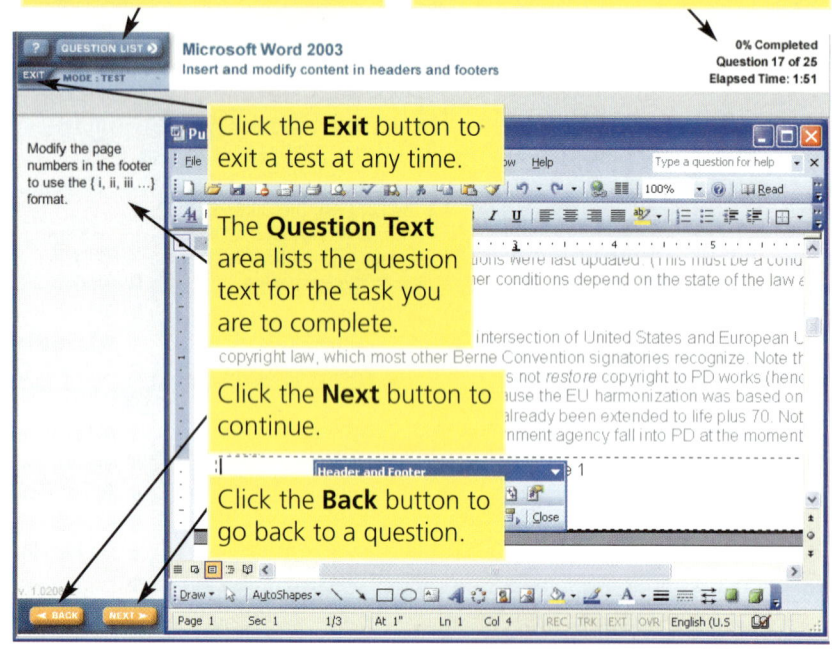

Click the **Exit** button to exit a test at any time.

The **Question Text** area lists the question text for the task you are to complete.

Click the **Next** button to continue.

Click the **Back** button to go back to a question.

Your instructor has many options on how to set up and administer a test, so you may find that options discussed below do not appear when you take a test. If an option is not available to you, it means that your instructor has not enabled this feature.

http://247.prenhall.com | 24

For example, if your instructor has set the test to allow multiple tries, after you complete a question, a message box appears, as shown in Figure 37. Clicking **Yes** returns you to the question to try again. Clicking **No** registers your answer and moves you to the next question.

Figure 37

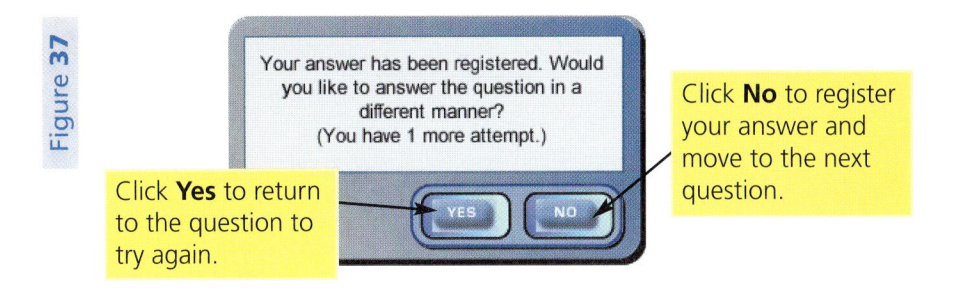

Your answer has been registered. Would you like to answer the question in a different manner?
(You have 1 more attempt.)

Click **Yes** to return to the question to try again.

Click **No** to register your answer and move to the next question.

Depending on how your instructor has set up the test, you also may see immediate feedback to tell you if you answered the question correctly or incorrectly, as shown in Figure 38.

Figure 38

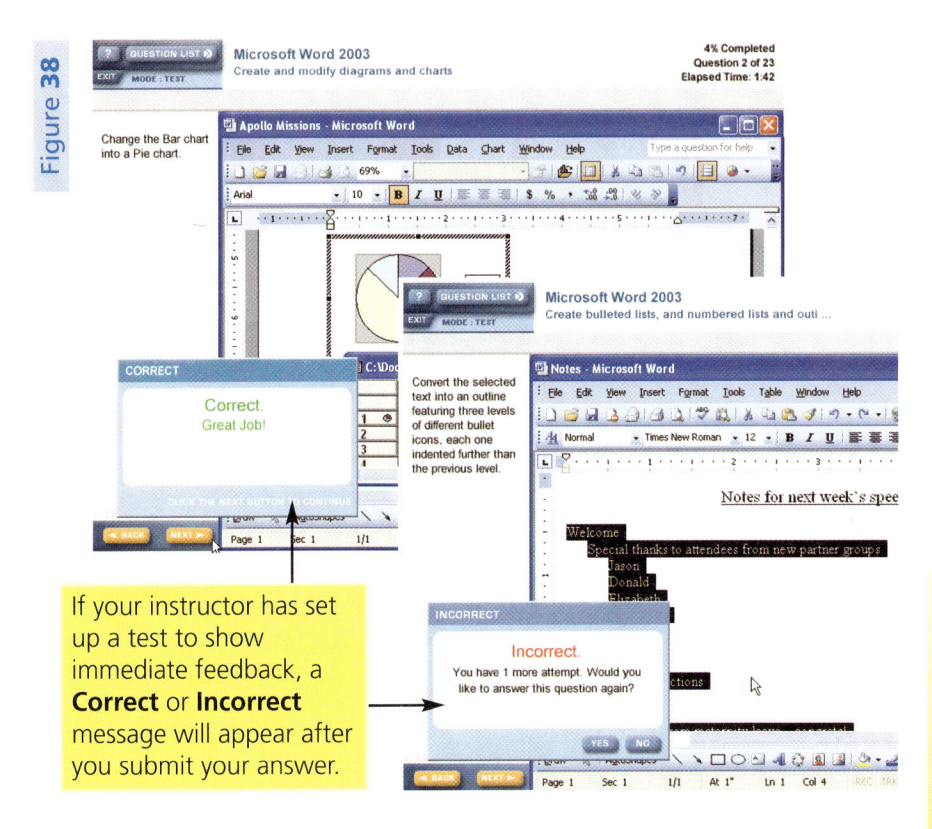

If your instructor has set up a test to show immediate feedback, a **Correct** or **Incorrect** message will appear after you submit your answer.

| user's guide

25

After you have completed the test or click the **Exit** button, you will be asked to confirm whether you want redo any questions or exit the test and register your score (Figure 39).

Figure 39

Click **Redo Questions** to revisit any questions that still have attempts remaining.

You have completed all questions in this test. Would you like to redo any questions or exit the test?

Click **Done** to exit the test and submit your score.

After you exit the test, if your instructor enabled this feature (Figure 40), a test results screen may appear. The screen provides summary test results information, as well as a detailed list of how you did on each test question. Clicking the **Exit Test** button closes this screen and ends the test.

Figure 40

Student Information lists summary test information, including percent correct.

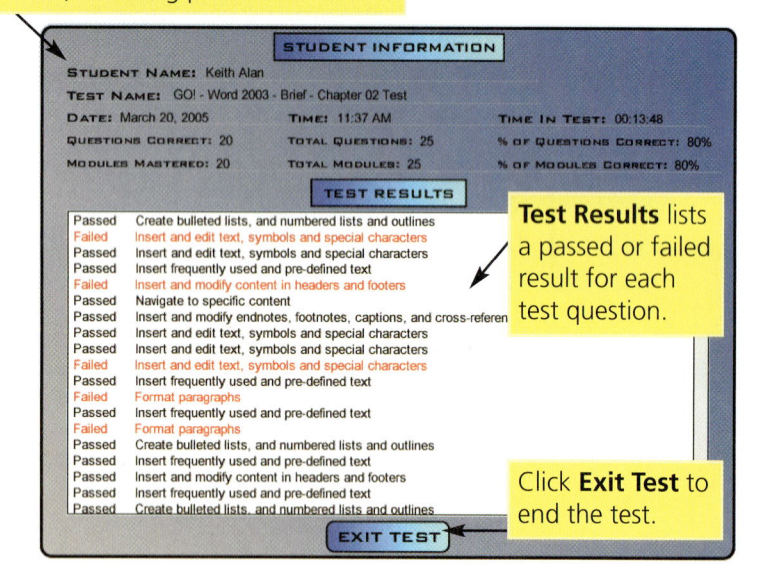

STUDENT INFORMATION
STUDENT NAME: Keith Alan
TEST NAME: GO! - Word 2003 - Brief - Chapter 02 Test
DATE: March 20, 2005   TIME: 11:37 AM   TIME IN TEST: 00:13:48
QUESTIONS CORRECT: 20   TOTAL QUESTIONS: 25   % OF QUESTIONS CORRECT: 80%
MODULES MASTERED: 20   TOTAL MODULES: 25   % OF MODULES CORRECT: 80%

TEST RESULTS

Test Results lists a passed or failed result for each test question.

Click **Exit Test** to end the test.

Using the Train IT CD

If you want complete training lessons without being connected to the Internet, you can use the Train IT CD or CDs in this package. To begin, insert the Train IT CD into your CD-ROM drive. The CD will start immediately.

Note: If the Train IT CD does not start automatically, complete the following steps:

1. Click the Start button.
2. Click Run on the Start menu.
3. Type **D:\start.exe** (where D is your CD-ROM drive).
4. Click the OK button.

Getting Help and Support

Train & Assess IT 3.0 provides several ways to get Help and Support while you are working, including the Student Guide and forms to contact your instructor or Tech Support.

Student Guide

The User's Guides page includes links to the Train & Assess IT Student Guide (Figure 41), which includes information on how to view available modules, training statistics, and messages from an instructor. The User's Guide also explains how to change your password, use the glossary, and contact Tech Support or your instructor for additional help. This guide can be accessed while in the program or can be printed out as a reference in PDF format (you will need Adobe Reader to view the PDF file).

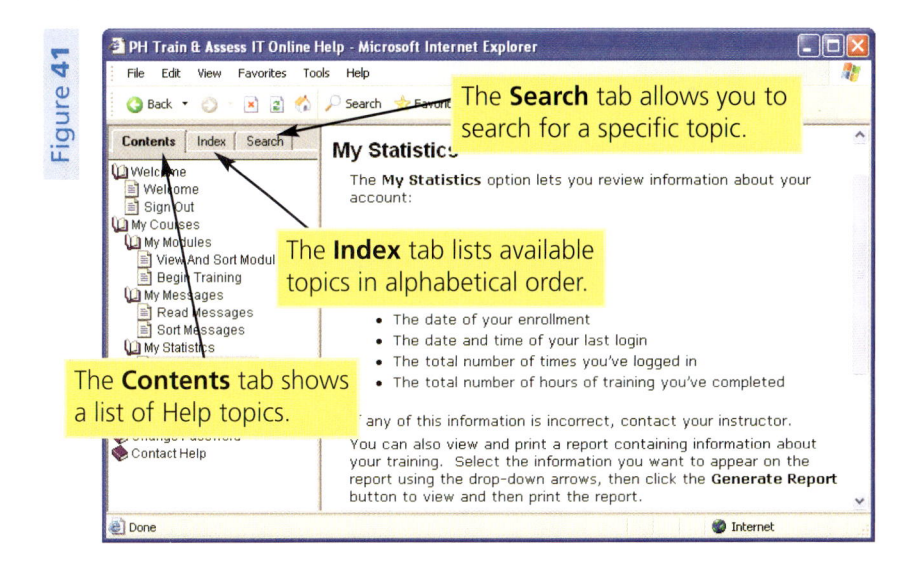

Figure 41

The **Search** tab allows you to search for a specific topic.

The **Index** tab lists available topics in alphabetical order.

The **Contents** tab shows a list of Help topics.

Contact Professor

The Contact Professor link allows you to send messages directly to your instructor, within the Train & Assess IT system. Clicking the Contact Professor link at the

| user's guide

27

bottom of the page opens the Message to Professor form (Figure 42). Enter your message and then click the **Send** button to send the message to your instructor.

Figure 42

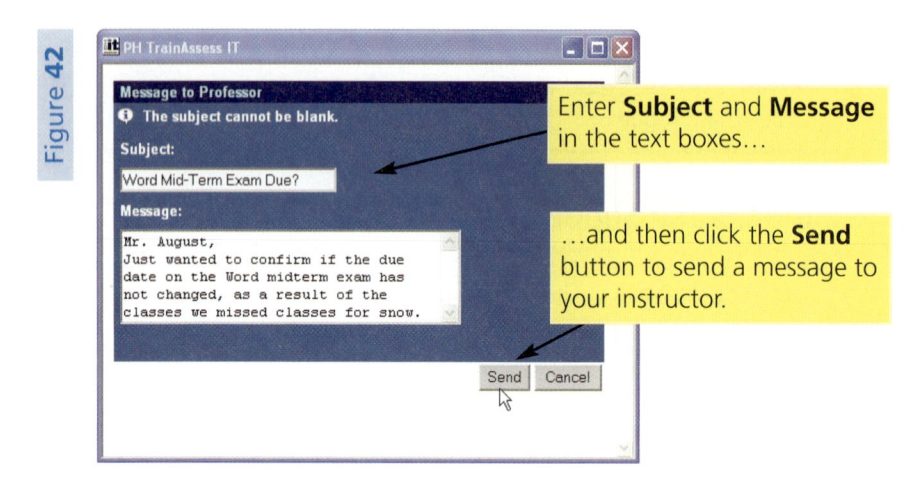

*Enter **Subject** and **Message** in the text boxes…*

*…and then click the **Send** button to send a message to your instructor.*

Contact Tech Support

You can contact Technical Support at any time, within the Train & Assess IT system by clicking the Contact Tech Support link at the bottom of the page. Clicking this link opens the Contact Tech Support form (Figure 43). Enter your message and then click the **Send** button to send the message to Prentice Hall Technical Support.

Figure 43

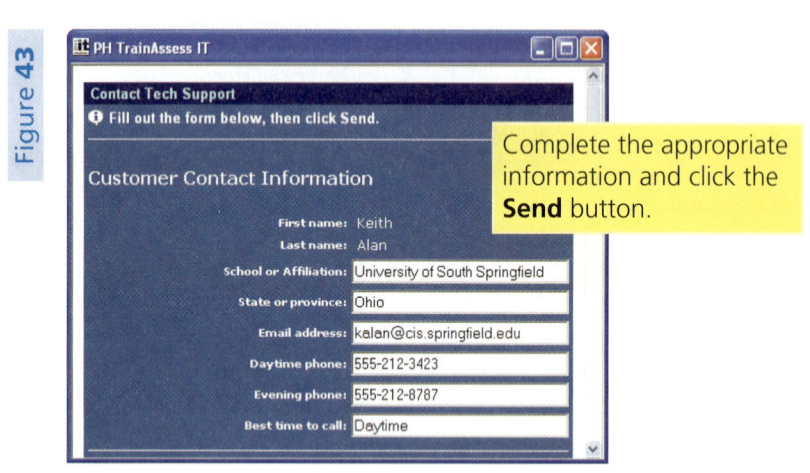

*Complete the appropriate information and click the **Send** button.*

You also can contact Prentice Hall Technical Support using the following information:

Student Technical Support

Web: 247.prenhall.com

E-mail: online.support@pearsoned.com

Phone: 1-800-677-6337

http://247.prenhall.com | 28